Julian Kennedy Smyth

Footprints of the Saviour

Julian Kennedy Smyth

Footprints of the Saviour

ISBN/EAN: 9783337314453

Printed in Europe, USA, Canada, Australia, Japan

Cover: Foto ©Lupo / pixelio.de

More available books at **www.hansebooks.com**

FOOTPRINTS OF THE SAVIOUR.

✠

Devotional Studies
in
The Life and Nature of our Lord.

✠

BY THE

REV. JULIAN K. SMYTH.

How beautiful upon the mountains are the feet of Him that bringeth good tidings, that proclaimeth peace; that bringeth good tidings of good; that proclaimeth salvation; that saith unto Zion, Thy God reigneth! — ISAIAH lii. 7.

BOSTON:
ROBERTS BROTHERS.
1886.

The Dedication.

LORD, my first fruits present themselves to Thee;
  Yet not mine neither: for from Thee they came,
And must return. Accept of them and me,
And make us strive, who shall sing best Thy name.
  Turn their eyes hither, who shall make a gain:
  Theirs, who shall hurt themselves or me, refrain.

HERBERT.

PREFACE.

————◆————

THIS little volume aims to make real to
thought and affection the Divine Humanity of
the Lord Jesus Christ. It does not attempt a
complete narration of the events in our Saviour's
life, neither does it seek to enter the forum of
critical discussion. Its purpose is, rather, to
present the Lord's Humanity in its saving relations to men; to show how real that Humanity
was, and how real it still is to all who are striving to understand their Saviour, and come within
the peaceful shadow of His Being. For unless
all signs fail, many are longing to understand the
unity of God in Christ; and the tempted and
the penitent, the weary and the heavy-laden,
would fain cast themselves upon His blessed
Personality, and find rest unto their souls.

The chapters which follow are written from a religious point of view which, it is believed, makes plain the divinely human nature of the Lord, to the end that faith may look to Him with cleared vision, and that love may cling to Him in humbleness of heart. For to how many a would-be disciple could Christ say, as He once said to Philip: "Have I been so long time with you, and yet hast thou not known Me?"

Boston, October, 1886.

CONTENTS.

THE FOOTPRINTS.

And He hath said, How beautiful the feet!
The feet so weary, travel-stained, and worn, —
The feet that humbly, patiently have borne
The toilsome way, the pressure and the heat.

With weary human feet, He, day by day,
Once trod this earth to work His acts of love;
And every step is chronicled above
His servants take to follow in His way.

L. G. Stock.

The Footprints.

✠

" I will make the place of My feet glorious."

✠

IT can never be forgotten that it was by the feet that the company of women held our Lord and worshipped Him on the great day of Resurrection. "All Hail!" He said to them as they hurried to tell the disciples of the empty sepulchre. "And they came and held Him by the feet and worshipped Him."

And they were not the first to bow there. Simon Peter had knelt there when the divinity of his Lord came upon him with such overwhelming power that he could only cry, "Depart from me, for I am a sinful man, O Lord." Jairus, ruler though he was, came and fell at His feet; for his little daughter was dying, and he needed help and comfort. Many a time the people brought those that were lame, blind, dumb, maimed, and many other afflicted ones, and, in the language of one of the Gospels, "cast them down at Jesus' feet; and He healed them." The Syro-phenician woman, with spirit so humble that she was content to be likened unto one of the dogs which eat of the children's crumbs, came and fell at His feet and begged for the healing of her daughter. When the devil-legion had been cast out of the man of Gadara, the people hurried out of the city to see him; and they found him "sitting at the feet of Jesus, clothed and in his right mind." More touching still must have been the sight of the penitent woman in the Pharisee's house. A woman of shame she was, yet stole to where the Saviour was reclining; and though the Pharisee had nothing but scornful looks and cutting words, she kissed and anointed the feet of Him who came to call sinners to repentance. At those feet pious Mary sat, listening to His words with such rapt attention that she forgot her sister, fretted with "much serving."

One simple but impressive fact comes to us from these and similar incidents, — the Lord received and accepted men's reverence. True, very many utterly rejected Him. Many thought of Him only as a good man. But we cannot forget that there were some — no matter how few — who felt that He was more than a good man or a prophet even. There were some who felt that their place was at His feet. And yet to all outward appearances the Lord was there as one of them. He told them, indeed, who He was; but it must have puzzled them sometimes to see Him living on their plane and amid their conditions.

Now, if He had come with signs of supernatural glory; if He had appeared only to their spiritual sight, as John once saw Him, His eyes as flames of fire, His face shining as the sun, His feet like unto polished brass; or as the three apostles saw Him at the transfiguration, a figure of dazzling brightness, — if the Lord had come in any such way, we should never have thought to ask why people knelt to Him.

But He did not come in this way. The Humanity He assumed grew up in plain sight of all. He lived for thirty years in the little village of

Nazareth. At length He goes forth. He bids men follow Him, not as a reformer, or a new philosopher, but as the Christ, the " Anointed," the Word incarnate. He performs miracles. He teaches with an authority that belongs to no man. He forgives sins. He stills the tempests. He raises the dead. And yet outwardly He lives a human life, subject to fatigue, hunger, pain, death. He places Himself, on one occasion, in the attitude of a servant, bending over the feet of His twelve apostles, — not excepting the man who lifted up his heel against Him. He says to them, "I am among you as one that serveth." But still a certain something, which was not of earth, nor of man, flowed out from that Humanity and brought men to their knees. In short, they knelt to His Humanity as divine.

And this is a point of vast significance. We read the accounts of our Saviour's life. In our thoughts, we see Him as once He was seen by the organs of natural vision. Many things, of course, we do not see, — the look of His face, His dress, His deeds of miracle and love. But, speaking generally, we see Him in this wonderful presentation of Himself in His Humanity. And what do we see? One who was tempted and afflicted; One who mingled with the household life of fishermen and peasants; One who fasted and prayed, toiled and was crucified, yet presented Himself as divine.

Here is where many grow puzzled. This rock, the Divine Humanity of the Lord Jesus, divides their thought into two courses. They can think of Him with affection as one who was purely human. They are keenly sensitive to all that was beautiful, self-sacrificing, gentle, devoted in the life of His Humanity; always insisting, however, that to such a conception it is not only unnecessary, but positively confusing, to inject the quality of divinity. Perfect *man*, but not *God-man*.

And so, it is easy to see, the thought of God grows correspondingly more impersonal. God is thought of not so much as a person as an infinite power and essence, — an all-pervading something, penetrating and surrounding the natural universe; a supreme Order and Wisdom and Love, too infinite and far-reaching, it is claimed, to be centred in any being.

Thus, the stream once divided, its two courses flow wider and wider apart,— one towards man, towards the merely human; the other towards God, conceived of as infinite, divine, impersonal essence.

Let us look back, for a moment, to the Gospels. Did those who really believed in the Lord think of Him merely as man made perfect? The apostles were not theologians; and it was too early in the history of the Church to formulate an exact doctrine of the Son of Man. But it seems certain that the Lord encouraged them to believe that in some way within His Humanity dwelt the very divine Fatherhood; for He asked Philip, with a touch of disappointment, it would seem, as though it pained Him that he should have to be asked, "Believest thou not that I am in the Father, and the Father in Me?"

It is said in the Gospel of John,— and we hold to it strictly,— "No man hath seen God

at any time; the only begotten Son, which is in
the bosom of the Father, He hath declared [that
is, revealed] Him." Who can think of Divinity
as it is in itself? Who can comprehend Infinity,
—infinite love, infinite wisdom, infinite power?
Can any one? Is it not just this effort to try to
calculate these infinite powers and qualities, and
get some exact idea of them, that has baffled
and wearied many a brain, and made the existence of God seem such a hopeless thing for our
little intellects to grasp?

We throw ourselves upon these immense truths
of religion. God is infinite. His love knows no
bounds. His wisdom is unsearchable. His power
is exhaustless, — "For the Eternal One fainteth
not, neither is weary." But who can understand
such things? Our love gets so easily ruffled;
our wisdom becomes so easily clouded; our power
is so easily broken! Must God, then, remain as
this vast, incomprehensible Being, whose very infinity oppresses us? Can there be no accommo-
dation of Him to our finite perceptions? Can
He not bring Himself down in some way, and

show us something of that love and wisdom and power which, after all, we do rely on and wish to know more of? God in His own eternal brightness would blast our sight. But is there no veil upon which we can look without fear, and through which we can see His face? "No man hath seen God at any time," — that truth we know. But the other: "The only begotten Son, which is in the bosom of the Father, He hath revealed Him." Revealed Him how, — by telling us more about Him? But we cannot understand infinity. Let the astronomer tell us all he knows about the sun; we cannot look at it in its midday splendor: it only blinds our vision. We are finite, and always shall be. God is infinite, and always will be. And the point is not, educate the finite until it can grasp the Infinite; but let the Infinite reveal Himself in some form that is familiar to us, and which we can understand.

And that, the Gospels say, has been done through the Humanity of the Lord Jesus Christ. And what is necessary in order that that manifestation shall be a true and perfect one? Must not the

Humanity live from the Divinity, as the body lives from the soul? For how could any man, be he never so blameless, reveal in his own life the Infinite, which would be as hopelessly above his comprehension as above ours? Is it that once in the world's history there came a man pure and stainless, whose every act and every word were such perfect reflections of the divine love and wisdom that the world, as by one accord, could turn and say, " There, this perfect man has revealed God to us " ?

This, at least, is not what Jesus said. His claim was not that His Humanity was flashing back the divine brightness as from a mirror. The claim was a very different one. What was it? " The words that I speak unto you, I speak not of Myself; but the Father that dwelleth in Me, He doeth the works." In other words, the Divine is manifesting itself *through* the Human, not *upon* it. It is revealing itself from within.

And this is the only perfect revelation possible. The Human must be in such relations with the Divine that the Divine can be its life and soul, and not merely beam upon it. And because such a relation did exist, everything the Saviour said, everything the Saviour did, revealed the very Divine itself which we wish to know. The divine feelings of love were expressed in the love which Jesus showed for the world's salvation. He pitied men when He saw them in pain or trouble; He was kind, surely, to the unthankful and the evil; He was forgiving to His enemies, and prayed for those who despitefully used Him and persecuted Him. How quietly He labored in Nazareth! How gently He met opposition when He began to teach! How tenderly He dealt with sinners! How wisely He educated those who believed in Him, lifting them gradually upon higher planes of life! And now, think of all this as the revelation of God; think of it as the divine love and wisdom acting and speaking in a human way; think of the Humanity as God's Humanity, and how plain and beautiful it all becomes!

Do any ask of the divine love? Let them learn of it in the Saviour's love, as He kneels at

the grave of Lazarus; as He weeps over Jerusalem; as He blesses the little children; as He
heals the sick or comforts the sorrowful; as He
soothes the dying malefactor on the cross. Would
we know of the divine forgiveness? It is here
in this one sweet sentence of mercy: "Neither
do I condemn thee; go and sin no more."
Would we know of the divine activity? It is
all revealed in the sleepless nights of preparation,
spent alone on the mountains in prayer; the days
devoted to teaching and healing; the tireless
errands of mercy from village to village. Would
we know of the divine patience and endurance?
We have but to watch the calm, quiet way in
which He meets His betrayer and the company
that take Him; the false accusations, to which
He listens in silence; the ridicule, the taunts,
the blows dealt by savage hands, the coward-
ice of Pilate, the scourge, the thorn-crown, the
cross.

And so, we ask at last, would any know
God the Infinite? We point to His Humanity
and say: "He who invited the weary and the

heavy-laden to His breast; He whom even the winds and the seas obeyed; He who declared Himself ' the Way, the Truth, and the Life ; ' He whose spirit has inspired, comforted, ay, saved the struggling souls of men, — He, surely, is God-manifest."

" And it shall be said in that day, Lo, this is our God; we have waited for Him and He will save us : this is the Lord ; we have waited for Him; we will be glad and rejoice in His salvation."

Well may we rejoice. To know God, do we only have to come to Him in His Humanity ? Can we study Him, the things He did, the words He said, all breathing such mercy, all bound up so exquisitely with human cares and sorrows that it seems as if humanity must cling to Him ; can we go like the disciples and see where He dwelt, study as it were His footprints, — the contact of His life with earth and humanity, — follow Him from day to day, up the hills and down the valleys, through the fields and over the seas, until He becomes endeared to us as a person, and know that it is God in His Humanity we are following and beginning to love ?

Then we may well say in the words of old, " How beautiful upon the mountains are the feet of Him that bringeth good tidings, that proclaimeth peace ; that bringeth good tidings of good, that proclaimeth salvation ; that saith to Zion, thy God reigneth." The Lord was the bringer of good tidings, and He came proclaiming peace and salvation. His feet stood upon the Mount of Olives, as was promised. And they were beautiful indeed ! — coming down the mountains of love ; coming down and walking far into the valleys below, where man was toiling and suffering, a slave to sin. But the Prince of Peace came proclaiming salvation ; and His feet touched the earth where men were dwelling ; and His enemies pierced His feet ; but the print of them is not gone, for He had said in prophecy, " I will make the place of My feet glorious."

The traveller goes to those Eastern lands where the scenes of the Gospels are laid. The land is for the most part waste, and towns are but little

more than ruins. Yet he goes from place to
place; goes to Nazareth and to Bethlehem village ;
goes to "the little blue sea of Galilee," where the
fishermen were washing and mending their nets ;
goes to Jerusalem and sees the Mount of Olives,
whither the Lord frequently withdrew for the
night, and at its foot the garden of Gethsemane,
with the old olive-trees. And the thought
during his pilgrimage is, that he is in the land
which the Saviour trod, and among the mountains down whose slopes His feet walked when
He came proclaiming peace and salvation.

But there are other fields which bear His footprints, — the fields of our human life. These remain much as they were then. There are essentially the same cares, the same temptations and
sins, the same doubts and fears, griefs and sufferings, the same self-love. And God walked amid
these fields. His feet are His Humanity ; and the
print of those feet, the impressions left upon human life, can never disappear. "I will make the
place of My feet glorious," are the words of Him
who is Faithful and True. The footprints will

become plainer and brighter; and we shall try to walk in them. For, in the words of the apostle John, "He that saith he abideth in Him ought himself also so to walk, even as He walked." Then, indeed, would the promise come true, — "Yea, the Lord shall give that which is good, and our land shall yield her increase. Righteousness shall go before Him, and shall set us in the way of His steps."

THE CHRIST-CHILD.

Oh, my Child-God, most gentle King,
 To me Thy waxing glory show;
Wake in my heart as wakes the spring,
 Grow as the leaf and lily grow.

Thou gav'st Thy pure example so,
 The copy in my childish breast
Was a child's copy. I did know
 God, made in childhood manifest.

Long-suffering Lord, to man reveal'd
 As one that e'en the child doth wait,
Thy full salvation is my shield,
 Thy gentleness hath made me great.

Holy Songs, Carols, and Sacred Ballads.

I.

The Christ-Child.

✠

"And the Child grew, and waxed strong in spirit, filled with wisdom; and the grace of God was upon Him."

✠

IT was a hard, sinful world to which the Christ-Child came. Silently and at night, while the world slept, the Child Jesus was born. And when the dew was lifted, there upon the face of the earth lay the Bread of heaven! He came as peacefully as did the manna which fell upon the wilderness. *"Manhu?"* the children of Israel exclaimed, as they beheld "a small, round thing, as small as the hoar-frost on the ground, — "what is it?" *"Manhu?"* the world has continued to ask ever since "the living Bread" came down from heaven. There lies the Bread to be gathered from day to day and be "our daily bread."

"This is the Bread which cometh down from heaven, that a man may eat thereof and not die."

How simple to human sight, this Bread lying peacefully upon the world's wilderness! How sweet and strengthening to failing souls, who have tasted and seen that the Lord is good, and know that Jesus spoke truly when He said, "If any man eat of this Bread, he shall live forever."

But the Jews, we read, "murmured at Him because He said, I am the Bread which came down from heaven. And they said, Is not this Jesus, the son of Joseph, whose father and mother we know? How is it, then, that He saith, I came down from heaven?" What would they have said had they stood by the manger on the day of the nativity? What would they have said at any time during that childhood? Would they not have asked, with added scorn, how one who was born into the world apparently as other children, who grew in wisdom and stature as other children, could be this heaven-descended Bread?

Even Joseph and Mary were perplexed. When the shepherds of Judea came and told of "the flocks of God" which swept down

"And sang to them of peace,"

as though the heavens were trembling with joy and could not keep back the good tidings, "Mary kept all these things and pondered them in her heart." When the devout Simeon took the Child in his arms, as it was brought into the temple, and blessed God, saying that he had at last seen the salvation prepared before the face of all people, "Joseph and Mary marvelled at those things which were spoken of Him." They could not have forgotten what angels had said of Him. They knew the promises of their Scriptures. Yet still they marvelled.

Down into Egypt they fled, to save this young life from the murderous hate of Herod. They take Him to Nazareth; and there in that despised little town, unknown, unnoticed, it may be, "the Child grew and waxed strong in spirit, filled with wisdom, and the grace of God was upon Him."

3

At length the time came when, according to
Jewish custom, He must go up to the Passover
at Jerusalem. Up to the age of twelve, Hebrew
parents were regarded as responsible for a boy's
conduct, and they had absolute control of his
ritual performances. But after twelve, they were
required to present him to the Lord. The boy
was inducted as member into the community
amid solemn and impressive ceremonies. He
then became what was known as a "son of the
Law."[1] So we read of our Lord, "And when He
was twelve years old, they went up to Jerusalem,
after the custom of the feast."

It is pleasant to think of this first Passover
as agreeing quite closely with our first Communion, and of the induction as a son of the
Law as similar to our rite of Confirmation.[2]
It is pleasant to think that the Lord has gone
before us in this way; that there was for Him
a first Passover, and an entrance upon the religious responsibilities and duties of youth.

The week of the feast is ended, and the many

[1] See Note A.   [2] See Note B.

thousand pilgrims set out for their homes. At the
end of a day's journey Mary and Joseph discover
that the Christ-Child is not in their company, as
they had supposed. Three days they search for
Him, and then they find Him in one of the schools
of the rabbis, held in the temple courts, with the
doctors and, most likely, their pupils gathered
around Him. The Scripture is that day being
fulfilled, which says, "I have more understanding
than all my teachers; for Thy testimonies are
my meditation. I understand more than the
ancients; because I keep Thy precepts."

For Mary and Joseph, the mystery of this
young life is deepening. A son, yet not a son.
Dutiful, it would seem; gentle, submissive; He
is with them but not of them. How plainly this
is brought out in His answer to Mary. She
appeals to Him half reproachfully, "Thy father
and I have sought Thee sorrowing." There is
parental authority in the appeal. "Thy father
and I," — Joseph and Mary. And how does
He answer? A few words gently reminding the
woman of a divine Fatherhood she should not

have forgotten — "Wist ye not that I must be about My Father's business?"

It surely is a most expressive figure, this lad from Nazareth, standing there amid the teachers of the Law, breaking away from the past, looking into vistas of truth which were opening upon His clearing vision; and then the woman and the man clinging to Him as their own. "My Father's business." He will go back to Galilee; He will toil as one of them; He will be known simply as "the carpenter;" but whether in Nazareth or in Jerusalem, whether in the house of Joseph and Mary or in the temple, whether in the carpenter's shop or in the school of the rabbis, a divine mission, a divine connection with an indwelling Father is growing and growing, bringing Humanity and Divinity into relations which can best be described as those of Father and Son.

Many keep coming back to this figure with no slight perplexity. Later on when we see Him in the full exercise of His wisdom; later on when we see Him healing, blessing, forgiving, touching with saving power the sinking spirits of men, we seem to come more fully into the meaning of His life. When the time comes that He can declare Himself the very light and life of the world; when He can invite the disconsolate to His breast; yea, when He can spread His arms upon the cross in one last act of self-sacrifice, we can more easily enter into the truth of His declaration, "I am in the Father, and the Father in Me." We can see and feel how perfect the love is; how transcendent the wisdom is; how saving the power is; and seeing and feeling these things, make Him the supreme object of our faith.

But back there is the Child of Nazareth, growing and waxing strong in spirit much like other children. There is the lad come up to His first Passover, drawn, it would seem, both ways, — looking way beyond the things of earth, far above the temple, or the great city, or the rabbis, at the very moment that Joseph and Mary are claiming Him as their own.

Do we express what in some minds is a difficulty? Can anything be said which will explain how a human nature, conceived and born like the Son of Man, could go through the stages of physical and mental growth as we do, and yet be in personal connection with the Divine? If this be explained, is not everything of that most wonderful, and at the same time most comforting of all truths, the divinely-human nature of Christ, explained?

The subject is one which, in a sense, includes our own natures. A child is born. Perhaps all one can say of it is, that it lives. It is without thought. It is without conscious love. And yet it lives. And it lives differently from a plant. It lives differently from an animal. There is the delicate, tender body, — the little dimpled hands beating the air, the heedless, helpless, mysterious thing we call the baby. But within and above this outward, physical nature, there is an internal form, or principle, through which the divine life descends. By virtue of this principle, man is man and not brute, and capable of spiritual development. Being created, it is finite; and although it serves to admit the divine life, still it can only do so in a finite degree.

The child, however, is all unconscious of its inner soul-life. That can only come later. And it can only come at all, through the growth and development of the rational faculty, which is the great mediator between the soul and the body. We say "growth," because, as we know, a child is not born rational, but only with the faculty to become so.

And how does it become rational? Watch the development of a child, and we shall see how simple and beautiful the process is. By means of the senses, especially sight and hearing, the child comes into gradual possession of facts or knowledges. These knowledges keep increasing with every day. They become more various. And the point to be noted is, that they become the recipient vessels for the divine life, and for the introduction of higher forms of knowledge.

Take a simple illustration. We wish to teach a child about God. Suppose we should just say,

"There is a God." What would that convey
to him? Nothing, — absolutely nothing. We
are trying to give him a naked spiritual fact,
and he cannot understand it. Or suppose we
wish to tell him about the higher world, and
should simply say, " My child, there is a heaven."
What can that word " heaven" mean to him?
Nothing whatever.

But suppose we use simple forms of thought
in the child's mind. Suppose we begin with a
fact he knows from his child's experience, — his
father, — and then tell him of another Father,
who loves and takes care of us all; and suppose
from what he knows of this natural world, we tell
him about a beautiful, heavenly world, and of the
pure and beautiful children, and the angel men
and women there, — why, then we have done that
wonderful thing which we cannot do to any other
object in this universe: we have communicated a
spiritual truth.

These facts in a child's growth and rational development being recognized, we have the means of
understanding our Lord's divinely-human nature.

The Lord took upon Himself a human nature, with all the faculties for human thought and affection as a man, except in this : being conceived, as the Gospels declare, of the Holy Ghost, the internal of His Humanity was not a created form recipient of life, but *was* life. It was the Divine itself. And yet, can we not see that the Christ-Child, the nature born into the world, could have no consciousness of its divine soul? There would be that same hiatus between the inmost and outermost as with other children; and, as with them, it could only be supplied by the acquisition of knowledges through the senses.

We needlessly confuse ourselves if we think of the Babe in the manger as conscious of its Divinity; revolving mighty thoughts in its little brain; feeling the throbbings of infinite love in its child-heart. The time came when it had this consciousness in its fulness. But at first, the Child Jesus would be as another child. It would grow as another child, — grow, as the Gospels declare, in stature, in wisdom, and in grace. Only the incoming thoughts would crowd thick and

fast; the flux of love would be sweet and deep.
At twelve years He would have passed beyond
the wisdom of the doctors of the Law. Gradually His inner nature would be revealed to Him.
Each knowledge learned in the great school of
experience, every fact acquired by the senses,
would become a vessel for the treasures of infinite
wisdom. For it is a law of thought, that the
spiritual must rest upon the natural, like a temple upon its base. Silently, day by day, week by
week, the mind of the Human would, by the suc-
cessive development of all its degrees, become
more and more the temple of Jehovah. There
would be an overshadowing presence of the Divine, as of a father. A light from above would
fill the Humanity with a certain divine radiance,
until, in the days to come, Jesus of Nazareth
could calmly say, "I am the Light of the
world."

Is it not wonderful to think of the Humanity
of Christ accommodating itself to our condition
even in this : that it grew in knowledge in the
simple ways of a child; drank in, as it were,

the words of teachers, the scenes of Nature, and
the thousand facts of human life, because in
this way only could the Spirit of the Lord rest
upon Him, — the spirit of wisdom and understanding, the spirit of counsel and might, the
spirit of knowledge and of the fear of the Lord,
making Him of quick understanding in the fear
of the Lord.

Did the lad, looking, it may be, from that very
hill whence, a few years later, His enemies would
have cast Him headlong, watch "the keepers of
vineyards pruning their vines, the shepherds leading their flocks afield, the husbandmen sowing
their grain, the plains over which the breezes as
they swept made waves in the field of wheat and
tare, the reapers at their work over the vast sur-
faces of Esdraelon and El Battauf, the prognos-
tics of storm coming up from the sea, or of fair
weather when the sky at evening reddens over the
ridges of Carmel, 'the light of the world' coming out of the east to enlighten every man,"[1] —
did He look out on all these things? Full well we

[1] Sears's "Heart of Christ."

know that into all these scenes the divine wisdom flowed, and turned them into types which even now stand before our souls in lines of celestial beauty.

Those were wonderful years in Nazareth !

THE CARPENTER OF NAZARETH.

With musing long my heart doth yearn,
The silence of His youth to learn,
  The striving that His soul would stir.
By faith, by searchings, and by thought,
In Eastern sheds with Him I 've wrought,
  Many good days, a carpenter.

Holy Songs, Carols, and Sacred Ballads.

II.

The Carpenter of Nazareth.

✠

" Is not this the carpenter's son ? "
" Is not this the carpenter ? "

✠

THE reader, if he has seen Holman Hunt's "Shadow of Death," will remember that the picture represents the Master in the carpenter's shop at Nazareth. As He rests from His work, His position is such as to cast a shadow of the cross upon the background; and upon this, the shadow of death, Mary, who kneels near by, Mary, into whose soul the sword must enter, turns her face. The picture is one more attempt to fill up the blank spaces of those thirty years in despised Nazareth; to find the Messiah where the Gospels seem to lose Him; to interpret religiously that most obscure passage in the Master's life.

With many there is an evident desire to behold God in Christ, the Divine within the Human. We cling to the sinlessness, perfection, the infinitude of love, wisdom, and saving power, — this on the spiritual, divine side; and on the other, all those humanities and graces, the living and dying, which, at the end of nearly two thousand years, have still the power to smite and to console, to goad and to satisfy. Yet many feel that in speaking of the " Humanity of Jesus," or in showing that that Humanity fulfilled all man's conditions, not only in being born, but in physical, intellectual, and spiritual growth, His divinity is compromised; while others urge that every attempt to insist upon the supernatural origin and nature of the Redeemer is only to make His image less distinct, and retard His acceptance.

How like the story of old! Men and women offended, not because of the Redeemer's power and influence in the world; not because of the inspirations and consolations His name still brings; but offended because of this claim to divinity !

The people of Nazareth, crowding into their little synagogue to hear this new Teacher, did not for a moment think of denying either His power or His wisdom. The hardest and narrowest of them could but acknowledge that His doctrines were new and searching; nor could they deny what their own eyes saw. Up to a certain point they approved of Him. Up to a certain point they may have been proud of Him. As He finishes His discourse, a low exclamation of surprise escapes from the congregation. " Whence hath this man this wisdom, and these mighty works?" No one was there to say : This is not worth hearing ; these miracles are the merest trickery. Something in the bearing, the voice, but more than all, the truth uttered, must have impressed them too deeply for that. So all they could do was to question each other : " Whence hath this man these things ; and what wisdom is this which is given unto Him, that even such mighty works are wrought by His hands ?" Apparently they are on the point of going over to Him. A moment more, the cry of "Messiah" will

4

be on their lips. What hinders them? Why, this question: "Is not this the carpenter?" The tide has crept up to its highest mark. In a moment more it might have risen above that hard wall. Now it begins to recede. "Is not this the carpenter, the son of Mary, the brother of James and Joses, and of Juda and Simon? And are not His sisters here with us?" The enthusiasm is dying out fast. No matter now what He might say or do, they think they know Him too well. "And they were offended at Him." Telling words those! They were offended at Him because for thirty years they had known Him as a carpenter in Nazareth.

Look at the religious world to-day. Only the most shallow or the most conceited will deny beauty, wisdom, power, to this figure of the Lord Jesus. And after all has been said that can be said, after the critics have pruned the histories, and the cynics have sneered at our churches, and the unbeliever has gone over all his arguments by which he steels himself against spiritual faith, still the secret verdict of every thoughtful man who ever pondered the story of the Saviour would at least be that of Pontius Pilate, who found his first contempt changed into concern, — " I find in Him no fault at all." No fault at all! The teachings are lofty; the Teacher is sublime.

Why, then, do not all men accept Him? Because He presents Himself as something more than a Teacher. Because He says, "I came down from heaven." "The words that I speak unto you I speak not of Myself; but the Father that dwelleth in Me, He doeth the works." The world delights in heroes. And if Jesus of Nazareth were only a hero, a man with human antecedents, who felt the world's woes and vices so deeply that His soul became possessed with the one desire to ease it of its pains; to interpose His own pure nature between man and hell; not only to devote Himself, but to sacrifice Himself to the world's good; cure its sicknesses, solve its problems, guide its morals, — if no higher claim were put forth for Jesus of Nazareth than this, then, doubtless, the world would warmly receive Him. But this, we maintain, is the imaginary

Christ. This is the unhistorical Christ. This is the Christ of modern days. Where do we find this Saviour? Not in the Gospels; not in the Epistles; not in the writings of the Church Fathers. Place this Man-hero before the world, and we leave Him without a history.

Where was He born? In Bethlehem, do we say? Ah! but the very same record declares the divine origin of His birth, — the Virgin brooding over her motherhood; Joseph, troubled and conscientious; the shepherd folk; the Wise Men from the East. If one part is history, why not all? If the greater part is legendary, why not all? Yet there stands Bethlehem to this day; and here are our Christian Churches. What did this Man-hero do? Select some disciples? Truly; yet they called him Lord, and He said, " Ye say well, for so I am." What did He do? Preach the Gospel? Ay, and this was its great burden: "I am the Light of the world; " " I am the Way, the Truth, and the Life;" " Come unto Me, and I will give you rest." What did He do? Minister to the sick? Nay, we cannot break off here. He cured the sick with a touch, with a word; He raised the dead. What did He say? Read over His utterances and see how many of them we would put into the mouth of any man living or dead. Whom would we have say, "I am the Resurrection and the Life;" "I am the Bread of Life;" "He that hath seen Me hath seen the Father;" "all power is given unto Me, in heaven and in earth"? Strike out these and all similar declarations, and what have we left? Scarcely anything. The plan disappears. The unity and coherence are all gone. Nothing remains but a few isolated sayings. A Teacher robbed of His teachings! A Messiah with no solid plan of restoration!

Is not this a real dilemma? Christ the Saviour, honored, obeyed, not as He presented Himself, but as the critics have reconstructed Him; not as the early Christians declare He was, — and they sealed their testimony with their blood, — but as the people of the nineteenth century think He might have been! And what some think He might have been is simply this: The

Christ of the Gospels with the divine and the miraculous left out. And this, we hold, is nothing.

Why do any insist upon this? There are two reasons. First, because of a dislike to connect divine causes with outward effects. A universe creating and sustaining itself; man dependent upon his own human prudence and not upon Providence, — these are marked tendencies of our age. The other reason is a more worthy one; a real difficulty in understanding the union of the Divine with the Human. We say the Lord was divine; and yet we read of His being born; of His being subject to Joseph and Mary; of His dwelling thirty years in Nazareth, where He followed the trade of a carpenter. The religious mind instinctively asks: "Are such things compatible with the idea of God? Could God be born as a man? Could God become a child? Would God be a carpenter?"

Now, the Gospels reveal the Lord under what may appear to be two quite different, if not opposite conditions. There is Christ the child, the

boy of twelve years, the carpenter; Christ who
prays, toils, suffers; Christ who grows weary and
is tempted; Christ who touches the depth of human misery, and is crucified. And then there is
the Christ triumphant, — a Being speaking with
divine authority; looking far beyond the limits
of time; looking into men's souls; casting out
devils; forgiving sins; Christ the Saviour, high
above the littlenesses of men, unhurt by their
cruelties; "the Wonderful, the Counsellor, the
mighty God, the Father of eternity, the Prince
of Peace." Are these two conditions really op-
posed to each other?

Remembering our dual nature, the natural and
the spiritual, the one weak, halting, circum-
scribed, the other capable of the holiest thoughts
and impulses, — remembering this duality in ourselves, do we find it so inexplicable that the Saviour should reveal two natures, one quite like a
man's, the other infinitely above him?

Suppose for a moment it were possible that
a human nature could be born in all respects a
man except in this, — that its paternity should be

divine. This, it is objected, would be a miracle.
Certainly; but a miracle only in the sense that
it was unexpected and wonderful; a miracle perfectly possible, and in harmony with all the laws
of life, if God is the real though hidden source
of being.

Suppose, then, that in the Divine Providence
this creative life should of itself cause the birth
of a human nature. Born of a woman, it would
inherit the tendencies and characteristics proper
to man. It would be a nature requiring physical, intellectual, and moral growth. It would be
open to influences from without, that is, from the
natural world; and from within, that is, from the
spiritual world.

This human nature, then, in birth, in growth,
in all the daily experiences for good or evil, in
death even, would pass over the same road that
we are passing. The difference would consist in
this: that the soul animating that Humanity,
being uncreated, would be divine, — the Father
within the Son. And this would give the Humanity infinite possibilities for development. It

could grow infinitely in wisdom and grace. If it remained faithful, it could meet and overcome not only a few evils, as we may, but all evils. It could bear the assaults of the whole demoniac world, be tempted at every point, yet remain sinless.

Outwardly He would live the life of others. To human eyes, the carpenter of Nazareth would be as others; only more deeply thoughtful, and all unspotted. Inwardly, what thoughts, what perceptions! The salvation of the world opening up to Him! Deeper and deeper longings to live, suffer, and die for men's sakes!

At first, indeed, the Father within would seem high above the Humanity. But as that nature opened itself, the Divine would sweep down in glorifying measures. The consciousness of union would grow with each new experience. As with a man, the thoughts and feelings of heaven may work their way down to the very ultimates of his nature the more he resists evils as sins, until the very look on his face changes, so the thoughts, the love, the very heart of God would

gradually come into the Son of Man. The
Divinity would become merged in the Humanity. All that had been inherited from the
mother would day by day be put away. Then,
toward the last, the Son would become one
with the Father; and if any of His disciples
should ever say, " Show us the Father," He
could reply, " He that hath seen Me, hath
seen the Father."

Enemies might seize this all but divine body
and put it to death, but without avail. The
work would have been done. The Lord of heaven
would have made His way to men, would have
lived with them, thought with them, felt with
them. In a word, through the glorification of
an earth-born nature, He would have made His
Divinity human, and His Humanity divine.

Thus would be left upon the minds of men
an image of God-Man; and men could look and
pray directly to the Lord Jesus Christ as the
ever-present Saviour, within whom dwelt the fulness of the Godhead bodily, — Father, Son, and
Holy Spirit, one God in one Person; God in first

things and in last, in the highest and in the lowest, the one eternal Life-giver, the Sanctifier, the
Comforter, whom the great company of angels
worship and adore, crying, " Worthy is the Lamb
that was slain to receive power, and riches, and
wisdom, and strength, and honor, and glory, and
blessing."

What has here been set forth as a supposition,
will be maintained in what follows as a fact. The
further we go in the study of this most wonderful
life, the more surely shall we see traces of divinity
and of humanity, not as qualities which are opposite and irreconcilable, but capable of the most
perfect and absolute union. The Lord is divine,
— supremely divine, — or else in announcing
Himself as the Light of the world, the Bread
of life, the Vine in which we are but branches,
He has presumed too far upon our faith. And
since He was divine, we have cause to marvel
most that He could come to us in the simple,
humble way that He did. The people of Nazareth lost faith in Him, because they had known
Him as a carpenter. As we read the story over,

THE CHRIST.

Nor can the vain toil cease,
Till in the shadowy maze of life, we meet
One who can guide our aching, wayward feet
To find Himself, — our Way, our Life and Peace.
In Him the long unrest is soothed and stilled,
Our hearts are filled.

Helps by the Way.

III.

The Christ.

✠

" I am come to seek and to save that which was lost."

✠

W E desire, in this chapter, to set clearly before us the Saviour and His mission. His
childhood, and the years of simple toil in Nazareth, we have already considered. We have traced
in simple outline the growth of the Humanity,
which was assumed by incarnation, and shown its
relation to the Divinity from which it was living,
and with which it was being more and more
united. We have regarded this period as one
of solemn preparation, — a period in which the
Humanity went through the stages of physical
and mental growth common to man, and in which
it underwent deep spiritual struggles necessary to
its perfection.

We have now reached a deeply thrilling period. Thirty years have passed away in works of love and lowly service. In the midst of His toil or in moments of rest, in the home of Mary or out among the industries of men, the consciousness of His divine power has deepened, and His mission has been fully unrolled. He has heard " the groaning of the prisoner," and He has yearned " to loose the children of death." He has seen their sinfulness; He knows the darkness of their ignorance. Their sorrows are upon Him; their pains have entered Him. He longs to go forth to save, " to bind up the broken-hearted, to proclaim liberty to the captives, and the opening of the prison to the bound: to proclaim the acceptable year of the Lord; . . . to comfort all that mourn."

At length He issues forth. What were His words to the little family as He passed out of the village, how He went, whether alone or in company with others, we know not. His entrance upon His ministry was as simple and as quiet as His entrance into the world. Not as a Philoso-

pher, with band of scholars to follow Him; not
as a powerful Hero, setting out amid the cheers of
admiring crowds to win laurels of earthly victory,
did He go forth. It was only the "Anointed,"
the "Good Shepherd," setting out without pomp
to seek and to save the lost.

He bends His steps towards Bethabara, where
the Jabbok empties its waters into the Jordan.
As He nears the ford, large numbers of people
are seen coming from all directions towards the
spot, — "fishermen from Galilee, shepherds from
' beyond Jordan,' vine-dressers from Judea, publicans from Jericho and Capernaum, soldiers going
to war against the King of Arabia, proud Pharisees and scornful Sadducees from Jerusalem."
For four hundred years no prophet had been
seen in Israel. But now a man had at last been
"sent from God," — a man so clearly beyond and
above his age, so stern in his denunciations of sin,
so scornful of hypocrisy, so peremptory in his
summons to "repent!" that his words sounded
with an unearthly ring; and the news was spread
far and near that Elijah, or one of the prophets,

had appeared upon the scene. There he stood, with the dress and appearance of one of the prophets of old, with bronzed features and un-shorn locks, his raiment of camel's hair, and a leathern girdle about his loins. And as the multitudes gather about him, some of them demanding of him who he is, some questioning his authority to baptize, he tells them of the coming of One so far above him, so pure and immaculate, that he declares himself unworthy to perform even the slave-boy's service of unloosening the thongs of his sandals.

Into this motley throng the Nazarene comes one day. In full sight of all He descends into the waters of the Jordan, that He may "fulfil all righteousness;" and as He comes forth the heavens are opened, and lo, a voice, saying, "This is My beloved Son, in whom I am well pleased."

Forty days elapse, and then this same gentle Being comes forth from the wilderness and is again pointed out by the Baptist, who hails Him as "the Lamb of God." Five men — probably

John's disciples — join Him, and own Him as their
Master. And He, instead of taking a path par-
allel with the asceticism of the desert preacher,
bends His steps towards a marriage festival,
where life is flushed with love.

And now, we seem to have the figure of the
Christ fairly before us. We have before us One
whose Humanity is, by incarnation, similar to our
nature, capable of sorrow, temptation, and suffering, but whose inmost soul is the Divine itself,
with which it is coming into closer and closer
union, — a Being so tender and merciful that there
is nothing of pain or humiliation which the meek
and the lowly One will not bear; so absolutely
pure and true, that beneath every indignity or
cruelty we shall see His divine majesty and glory.
Men's blows will only prove how enduring He is;
and the crimson drops upon His visage, from
what infinite depths His love is flowing; and the
crown, spiked upon His brow, will tell of a kingdom as high above the dominions of this world
as the heavens are high above the earth; and the
cross will flash and flash again with glory.

And what has the Christ come forth to do? For at the outset we must recognize that He had a mission, — a mission so deeply and perfectly laid, so clearly seen, that He never swerved from it. It is crowding upon Him when, at the age of twelve, He says to Mary and Joseph, "Wist ye not that I must be about My Father's business?" It is upon His heart when, in later years, He says, "I must work the works of Him that sent Me." "I cast out devils," is His message to Herod, "and I do cures to-day, and to-morrow, and the third day I shall be perfected." "Behold," He says to the disciples, His eyes fixed upon the closing scenes of His ministry, "we go up to Jerusalem: and the Son of Man shall be betrayed unto the chief priests and unto the scribes, and they shall condemn Him to death, and shall deliver Him to the Gentiles to mock, and to scourge, and to crucify Him: and the third day He shall rise again." He saw it all; for He knew, better than His enemies, all that the Scriptures had said of Him; explaining to His disciples many of the prophecies with reference to

Himself, and rebuking Peter's bold attempt to rescue Him in the garden, by saying, " How, then, shall the Scriptures be fulfilled, that thus it must be ? " It is of a mission which has never for one moment been lost sight of, that He says at the close of His ministry, " I have finished the work which Thou gavest Me to do."

Who ever planned a mission as this was planned? Who was ever so true to it? Our best intentions may never gain realization ; time will reveal defects in all our work ; we may have to try new methods, or modify our aims. If our life is an earnest one, and we are struggling for high ends, we shall more than once falter in the strife, and in the face of obstacles seemingly insurmountable be tempted to give up in despair. But at the close of that most tried and afflicted ministry, the Son of Man could say, "I have finished the work which Thou gavest Me to do." The work has been perfectly performed, because the end was so high, and the means so true, and the endurance so divine, and the self-sacrifice so absolute. In a few hours more His work will

seem to be undone; for He will hang upon a
cross, and His enemies will compass Him about
like dogs, and defy Him to assert His power.
But He expires with the cry of perfect victory on
His lips: "It is finished!"

This, also, is to be considered: the Saviour
did not simply have previsions of His death;
He came to die. It was part of His divine
plan. Differently from every martyr before or
after Him, He had the power to lay down His
life and the power to take it again; yet in the
very consciousness of this power, He chose to die.
And although His enemies appeared to overpower
Him, His words were strictly true: "No man
taketh My life from Me, but I lay it down of
Myself."

What, then, did the Christ come forth to do?
We state three great objects of His mission.

1. The Lord came to redeem men from the
tyrannous power which evil spirits were wielding.
"He that committeth sin," He said, "is the servant of sin;" and the world, through long-
continued evil, had reached a point of servitude so

absolute, that the very power to resist evil was
slipping away, exposing the race to the dominion
of the infernal worlds. It was, therefore, a truly
fearful moment when the Son of Man was
"tempted of the Devil." Could evil spirits, by
subtlest wiles or show of force, overcome Him,
or swerve Him from His purpose, the world was
lost. If, on the other hand, He could overcome
any and every form of evil they could devise; if
their attacks upon His love, — their attempts to
animate Him with a desire to use force and
over-ride man's freedom, to condemn His enemies, to vindicate Himself, to change His purpose, be it by never so slight a degree, anything,
in a word, which would have taken from the
perfection of that love, — if He could resist all
such attacks, be tempted at every point, yet
without sin, then, surely, He would lead captivity captive, break up this monstrous tyranny,
and bring the realms of darkness into such a
condition of order that man would at least be
free, henceforth and forever, to choose his own
destiny. And this, as we shall hereafter show,

the Redeemer accomplished; not simply by the
thrice-won victory in the wilderness, but by His
continual resistance and conquest of evil.

2. But this work of redemption, or restoration to spiritual freedom, momentous as it was,
was not the only work that was accomplished.
The Son of Man came also to save. It is not
enough to strike the fetters from a bondman's
limbs. For with his freedom come great responsibilities; and unless he be helped and educated
to bear properly those responsibilities, of what
avail is his freedom? "Behold, thou art made
whole," the Saviour said to the impotent man
whom He had healed; "sin no more, lest a
worse thing come upon thee." For thirty-and-
eight years the man had been lying helpless and
forlorn. Now he had his strength and freedom;
but his new life involved him in greater responsibilities than before. The Christ, therefore,
came not only to redeem, but to save. Let us
note carefully what He did to become a Saviour.

(a) And first, we can but notice the power of
His divinely-human presence. From the moment

that He enters upon His ministry, He presents
Himself as One who is worthy of man's best
faith and love. The people saw among them a
Being supremely good. They felt that, and it
touched them; it awed them. He impressed
them as a true, kind friend, rather than as a
philosopher, and it strengthened their confidence
in Him. They could but feel how real His life
was. They could see Him in their market-places,
in their synagogues, amid their fields, on the lake
in company with their fishermen. His home was
the world and its people; His themes, the cares,
the temptations, the moral and spiritual sicknesses of men; His promises, deep peace of heart
and life eternal for all who would resist evil as
sin and keep the commandments. They knew
He was far above them in wisdom and holiness.
Yet there He was, sharing their existence, healing their sick, blessing their little children, sitting
at meat with those whose very touch would have
been a defilement to the religious leaders. They
knew His power, and heard Him say that at a
word bright phalanxes of angels would rush to

His rescue. Yet they saw Him suffer His enemies to arrest Him, to bind Him, to strike Him, to spit upon Him, to nail Him to a cross, to mock Him in those last dark hours. Could such condescension and mercy, such self-restraint, fail to touch them? And after the resurrection and the ascension into heaven, when His divinity and glory were no longer doubtful, think how it would affect them to look back in remembrance over those strange, hallowed years, when He dwelt so simply and lovingly among them. How the sinner and the slave would listen to the accounts of such a Saviour! How that life of self-sacrifice would warm and stir their hearts!

(*b*) In addition to His loving presence, we note the saving power of His truth. We do not simply mean that everything which the Saviour said was true, that His teachings were sublime, and that they will ever underlie the best and purest civilizations. It was not truth in the abstract, which He gave to men. That might only have found its way to the schools and the academies, and even there become merely the subject of speculation and debate. The Lord's truth has power because He was Himself the Truth, — the Word made flesh. It cannot be separated from Him. It is Himself. He taught no truth which He did not Himself fulfil.

"A new commandment I give unto you," He said to the disciples, "that ye love one another; as I have loved you, that ye also love one another." Observe that the Lord bases this "new commandment," which shook the world to its centre, on His own experience, or life. It was not altruism in the abstract, concerning which one might speak or write from the standpoint of a cold and remote philosophy. "*As I have loved you,*" — that was the truth. The Saviour had said very little to the disciples about His love. He had simply loved them; and they knew it; they could not forget it; it was truth to them.

He would teach them the dignity of service; for they had been disputing among themselves for the chief seats at the supper. What does He do? He rises from His place without a

word, arrays Himself as a servant, takes a basin
of water, and performs the menial duty of washing their feet.   He made honest service a truth
to them.   The act — the sight of their revered
Master bending before them and laving their feet
— smote them as no words could have done.

In the truth of the Saviour, therefore, there
is the power of a divinely loving life.   And every
word He spoke, every principle of holy, Christian living He announced, was the exact expression of what He fulfilled in His own nature.

(c) Something more the Saviour came to give
to men, — something without which the recol-
lection of His life, or the knowledge of His
truth, would have been of little avail ; that
"something" which He signified when, after His
resurrection, He breathed upon His apostles,
saying, "Receive ye the Holy Spirit."   The
Spirit of the Saviour, flowing from Him in His
divine and glorified Humanity, to quicken men
to repentance, and to sanctify and strengthen all
who would open themselves to His influence, —
this, surely, is one of the fruits of His sacred

ministry on earth. And the spirit of mercy, of truth, of self-sacrifice, whenever it moves the souls of men to-day, is the Spirit of Christ, who is still abroad seeking and saving the lost, drawing them to Himself, according to His promise: "And I, if I be lifted up, will draw all men unto Me."

> "I sought the Lord, and afterward I knew
> He moved my soul to it Who sought for me;
> It was not I that found, O Saviour true;
> No, I was found of Thee."

3. One purpose more we notice as belonging to Christ's mission: the establishment of a universal brotherhood among men. Under the figure of the Good Shepherd preserving His flock, unwilling that even one should stray alone among the mountains, the Lord told the world how He was yearning to bring all men together and keep them under His pastoral care. "One fold under one Shepherd," was His prayer. In His doctrine of love, which so entirely does away with class distinctions, there being but one Master, even Christ, all men being brethren, a certain power

of union was instantly felt, which drew men together in loving and spiritual communions. Remembering how He had shared life with others, how He overlooked no one, how the poor and the sinful were dear to Him, the early Christians found "how good and how pleasant it is for brethren to dwell together in unity." "A new voice was heard: a new yearning upon earth, man pining at being severed from his brother, and longing to burst the false distinctions which had kept the best hearts from each other so long, — an infant cry of life, — the cry of the young church of God." Yet the cry was but an echo of that of the Saviour Himself, who, yearning for the spiritual unity of all men, prayed, "that they may be one as we are." Instructed and guided by the same Scriptures; coming together in the same Sacraments; looking to the same Saviour, — these Christian communities derived unwonted strength through their spiritual fellowship. And while we know that unholy ambitions and false teachings invaded the Church, and "the abomination of desolation" stood in the place where it ought not, we should also know that the Lord is still in the effort to unite mankind in one holy bond of faith and charity. And not until sectarian strife is hushed, and church rivalries are dead; not until faith and charity shall be united; not until the pride of wealth and fashion and numbers is scourged from the temple, and the salvation of man, be he high or low, rich or poor, wise or ignorant, be the one great impulse throbbing within the Church of the Saviour, — not until then will mankind be welded into that great Christian brotherhood, that universal kingdom of truth and love, which, when it comes, will be the coming of the kingdom of the Lord.

This life, whose mission we have merely outlined, we seek to know. In the belief that the Lord Jesus Christ is the Light of the world, and that His life is the light of men, we endeavor in what follows to make Him real to our thoughts and affections. For He Himself said, " Take My yoke upon you, and learn of Me." He placed Himself before the world that we might learn

of Him; He accommodated Himself to men's
conditions — lived with them, labored for them,
died among them — that we might follow Him
step by step; be touched by His gentleness; be
sanctified by His sanctity; be melted by His
self-sacrifice; and so, little by little, acquire deep
love for Him, and find that for us who toil, and
become "weary and heavy-laden," and suffer
pains of heart and of conscience which cast us
down, He is what no one else can be, — our Way,
our Truth, our Life.

THE SYMPATHY OF CHRIST.

Saviour, shed Thy mercy o'er us;
  All our weakness Thou dost know;
Thou didst tread the earth before us,
  Thou didst feel its keenest woe:
Lone and dreary, faint and weary,
  Through the desert Thou didst go.

Edmiston.

IV.

The Sympathy of Christ.

✠

" For He knoweth our frame ; He remembereth that we are dust."

✠

OUR theme is a tender one. We should also find it a far-reaching and a helpful one. We may apply other attributes, — sinlessness, gentleness, self-sacrifice, patience, wisdom, majesty, — but unless there is a truth in the sympathy of Christ, there is a craving in us left unsatisfied. For in sympathy all these other qualities are, as it were, gathered up and made to minister to the needs of our humanity.

Have we never reflected how powerless for the development of the highest qualities of good the divine life would be without this element of sympathy? Every presentation of God as a stern, distant monarch, scrutinizing our thoughts and actions with piercing, omniscient eyes, prompt to visit every transgression with its exact measure of punishment, — as though He were more intent on the maintenance of His law and of His majesty than the condition of the transgressor, — this cannot but have a depressing and suppressing influence. Under conditions like these, one could never get beyond the timid obedience of a servant; and however exact his obedience might be, he could never rise above the feeling that God was following him with an accusing eye, pursuing rather than defending him, ready to punish rather than befriend him; and so feeling, never rise out of the life of fear into that of love. Allegiance under such conditions is a dread and a despair.

We do not say that fear has not its place. With a stiff-necked and rebellious people the government of law and fear is a necessity. Only the result remains the same. The religion of fear never carries its disciples beyond the life of outward obedience, — that obedience which the trained servant renders to a rigorous master. It does not, it cannot bring them into sympathetic friendship, in which there is a closeness of soul through love. It is well that "the Law was given by Moses," but, blessed be God, "grace and truth came by Jesus Christ." And when Christ said to the men about Him, " A new commandment I give unto you, that ye love one another ; as I have loved you, that ye also love one another," it was as much as to say that they could step out of the religion of fear, and that instead of being mere servants of the divine will they could henceforth be friends with it; for the time had come when He could take them into the life of the purest love, and let them feel His sympathy, — the sympathy of Christ.

Only we must understand what true sympathy is. Sympathy is not pity, although it is tender and pitiful. The apostle defines it when he says, " For we have not a High Priest which cannot be touched with the feeling of our infirmities, but was in all points tempted like as we are, yet without sin." In the apostolic sense, then, the sympathy of Christ is born of His sinless participation in the experiences common to the infirm humanities of men.

One may exercise pity without any partnership in suffering. We pity the heathen, not because we know of them through any experience, but because their uneducated, idolatrous condition appeals to us as a deplorable one. But where we have pity, the true missionary who has brought his life to theirs, entered into the shadow of their ignorances, prayed with them, spent himself for them, — he, surely, has sympathy. And in this kind of sympathy there is power, — the power of a loving life. And it is one of the beautiful dispensations of Providence, that out of the experiences which are common to us all we are enabled to minister to each other, as Christ ministered.

Suppose for one instant that we could have grown up without experiencing sorrow and temptation. Suppose we had grown up, as we seem to think we ought to grow up, without a pain, without a tear — happy from the moment we became conscious of our being. And now, suppose we should be forced for the first time to meet sorrow.

Death has entered our friend's household and taken away the treasure of his heart. But we know nothing of death, only life, — bright, thrilling life. Yet we go to him. We feel the unwonted pressure of the hand, as though the tremulous fingers had a language for such sad times; we note the look of pain, the swimming eyes, the sad, choking voice; and with it all the struggle to keep the grief back, and smile in the old familiar way. What could we say or do, sitting there in the face of sorrow, yet knowing nothing of sorrow?

Or suppose we had in some way lived out of the reach of temptation, and should now come upon it for the first time. A friend, we will say, comes and falters out his story. He tells us how evil came to him, and fascinated him, until he seemed to lose his reason and gave himself up to it. And he tells us, too, how the sin has stung him with shame. What a poor, helpless friend we should be to such a man!

But what a difference, in either case, if we could have met him in a sympathetic knowledge of his trials; if we, who had also known sorrow, we, who had also wrestled with temptation, could have taken the man's hand in ours, and answered its pressure as if to say, "I know something of what you are passing through, and from my own pained and tempted heart I feel for you and suffer with you"! Do we say there is no power in that? Must we not say, rather, that all the power which one life can communicate to another life comes through this medium of sympathy?

We do not forget that God is the true comforter and healer of wounded spirits. But God works through many agencies, — angels, the Scriptures, the Church. And one agency, surely, is man, — man made tender and sympathetic by what this life brings to us all. When we know that men around us are suffering, morally and spiritually; when we know that because of poverty, ignorance, and evil there is a degree of wretchedness from which we cannot and should not get entirely away; that the lives of men are tempted, and their spirits jaded, and they carry sorrows which only the people of God can carry, — ah, when we think of these things, is there not some-

thing beautiful in the fact that we, because we are
partners in one life, and have had the tides of joy
and sorrow, peace and temptation ebb and surge
through our members, can beckon for help one to
another and lend a hand when life needs the
touch of sympathy !

And now, if we apply this quality of sympathy
to Christ, do we not see what a tremendous truth
it carries with it ?   If Christ has sympathy such
as the apostle describes, it is because He, when
in the flesh, shared with men their life of labor,
trial, pain, temptation, and even death.   And this,
we are sure, is what Christians would feel.

If one should say, "The Lord has pity on
you," that does not reach our sorest need, if by
this we are only to believe that He, from His immaculate existence, looks down in commiseration
upon us, who stand at such an infinite distance
below Him ; looks down as if to say, "How poor,
and weak, and sinful you are ! how unlike Me !
how I pity you !" That is the religion of despair.   What comfort would there be in pity like
this ?   What inspiration in knowing that the

Lord measures His Being with ours; and because where He is perfect we are always imperfect, where He is loving we are selfish, where He is wise we are ignorant, should pity us as we would pity a worm?

But if we can feel that the Lord our Saviour has sympathy; if we will believe what a prophecy said of Him, — "He knoweth our frame; He remembereth that we are dust," and believing this, feel that it is not our distance He is calculating, but the nearness with which His Divine Humanity can come to the tempted humanities of men; if, relying on the saying of the apostle, we will remember that because Christ did participate in our life, and was tempted like as we are, He has direct access to our souls, and that His life flows down to us in tides of divine sympathy, then the sympathy of Christ becomes the very perfection of comfort.

Now, one significant fact which we cannot help noticing as soon as we begin this study, is that the Saviour Himself loved sympathy. "Will ye also go away?" He said to the apostles, when, having declared Himself "the Bread of life," many who heard that sermon gave Him up and left Him. The crowd grew thinner and thinner, until only the twelve were left about Him ; and, as though the time had come when even they would leave Him, He said, "Will ye also go away ?"

Or take His announcement on that last night in Jerusalem, when, out of the knowledge of what was to befall them all, He said, "Behold the hour cometh, yea, is now come, that ye shall be scattered, every man to his own, and shall leave Me alone : and yet I am not alone, because the Father is with Me." The time, the place, the form of the announcement, all seem to unite in telling us that their coming desertion was a sorrow to Him, and His human loneliness a trial.

And as though to leave us in no doubt, one touching incident is related. They have entered the garden of Gethsemane. The Lord takes Peter, James, and John, and having gone a little way with them, He says, "My soul is exceeding sorrowful, even unto death; tarry ye here and watch with Me." And going about a stone's cast away, He prostrates Himself in prayer. He comes back to where He left them, and finds them asleep; and bending over Peter (the man who was going to follow Him to prison and to death!) He says, "What, could ye not watch with Me one hour!" Already He was entering the shadow of that loneliness which nothing but the divine presence within could brighten; yet not without a pang of sorrow that not one of those men had a hand of comfort to give Him, but must sleep the time away! "And I looked," says an ancient prophecy, "and there was none to help; and I wondered that there was none to uphold."

Once more, — and this to show that the tenderness of the risen Saviour was as before. He comes to Peter, and to the man whose heart was saddened by such bitter memories He says, "Lovest thou Me?" Three times, even as He had been denied three times, He asks the question. And three times the tempted, troubled man replies, "Yea, Lord, Thou knowest that I love Thee."

Now, we are sure that in all these instances the Lord, in desiring the sympathy and love of His followers, desired it for a high end. For there is oftentimes among men a weak, an almost childish desire to be compassionated and loved; to feel that our cares, our welfare, our affection are of the greatest consequence. This comes largely from a merely selfish vanity. But our Lord's desire for sympathy was a holy desire, — a desire which expressed itself in these words towards the close of that great prayer on the eve of his crucifixion : " Father, I will that they also be with Me where I am." One in spirit, one in love, one even in the suffering of self-sacrifice; a sympathy of this kind, going out from the disciples to their Lord, and binding them by ties which nothing could break, — that is what Christ yearned for.

We look now at the other side of our subject, — the sympathy of Christ. That one should set himself to prove the sympathy of Christ would seem to be as uncalled for as to prove His Being. For what we must feel is, that His whole life was one of sympathy. He had sympathy for men individually, and in the mass. He looked over the multitudes that thronged about Him trying to touch Him, clamoring to be healed, and " He was moved with compassion on them, because they were tired and cast down, as sheep having no shepherd." Yet this did not prevent Him from feeling the frightened touch of an infirm woman, and healing her with the outflowing of sympathetic love. He could take the children in His arms and bless them; or sit at meat with publicans and sinners; or mingle His tears with those of Martha and Mary at their brother's grave; or bespeak forgiveness for the men who crucified Him; or soothe the sinking spirit of the dying malefactor by His side.

These, we recognize at once, are not rare instances indicative of one special quality, but are parts of one divinely-human, sympathetic life. But now what we wish to know is, Does this sympathy come down to us from the Lord in His glorified Humanity?

The seer of Patmos saw "One like unto the Son of Man." "But His head and His hairs were white like wool, as white as snow; and His eyes were as a flame of fire; and His feet like unto fine brass, as if they burned in a furnace." He heard those who were about Him praise Him; but it was no longer the fishermen of Galilee, in their homely dresses, but a multitude of the heavenly hosts, arrayed in white robes, and palms in their hands. And this was their song: "Blessing, and glory, and wisdom, and thanksgiving, and honor, and power, and might, be unto our God for ever and ever!" And we ask, From those angelic spheres, which seem so high because holiness is high, does the glorified Christ not simply think of us, but shed down His life to us, more powerfully even than our risen friends can do? Has He direct access to us in joy and sorrow, in labor, in sickness, in death? He is ascended where the material eye cannot follow Him; but is there nothing in His nature, or in the life He lived on earth, which binds Him to us with bonds of eternal sympathy?

7

Oh, we have heard Him described as standing alone above the universe of worlds, and from some dizzy peak of Paradise watching this spinning earth below, as though the mere fact of looking at us, and following our painful movements with His eye, could comfort us ! But our faith should be, that the Saviour Christ does not merely gaze upon us ; but that from the nature of His. Divine Humanity, and from the urgency of His love, He is among us by the Spirit of His love and wisdom ; among the wrecks of life everywhere ; among our industries, our temptations, our births and deaths; in and out through the doors of the soul, with as much power for help, did we but lay hold of Him, and as much sympathy as when men knew Him only as the Nazarene, who went about in His calm, heavenly way doing good.

Faith in the sympathy of Christ includes these great facts: that in the day of need the Lord God took upon Himself a human nature, lived in it, admitted into it the thoughts and feelings of men; that He united His Humanity to the Divinity within, and thus glorified it, that is, made it divine; that through the Incarnation, with all the experiences it brought, there is added to the divine nature this plane, or degree, of human life which was sanctified; and that it is through this Humanity — the Humanity of God — that the divine love and wisdom flow out to us. And since they issue from that Humanity, they come to us in forms accommodated to our simplest or our direst needs.

It was because God saw that men were getting farther and farther away from Him; that the inner doors of their minds were one after another closing against Him, so that a purely spiritual access to them was impossible; that the angels could no longer bring them His spirit; and that their very Scriptures had lost all effect, through their traditions, — it was because God saw all this, that He provided one more means for reaching and influencing them; took a human nature which could approach them from without; became the inmost of its life; gradually removed from it everything of an earthly or human origin, and as gradually brought the infinite, divine life into union with it, until, at the end, the Humanity itself became divine, and a very part of God, — that part which is next to us, and which cannot but be in sympathy with everything that is human. God is invested, if we may so say, with humanity. And from that Humanity, made perfect and divine through temptation and suffering, there issues a sphere of love and wisdom as real and as suited to our needs as the woman felt when she touched the border of His robe.

And why, to consider one point more, is the sympathy of Christ of such avail? We may say, "I have the sympathy of friends. I have the sympathy of friends and kindred passed beyond the limits and limitations of this earthly life. If sympathy comes from mutual participation in the experiences of our existence, why is there such unwonted power in the sympathy of Christ, seeing that others also have shared life with us?"

Turn back for a moment to the declaration of the apostle: "For we have not a High Priest which cannot be touched with a feeling of our infirmities; but was tempted in all points like as we are, yet without sin." *Without sin ;* and that which is sinless is divine. Who of us, ay, who from among any of the saints of earth could say, "I have been tempted in all points like other men, and without sin"? Who could say, "My sympathy for you is a sinless sympathy"? And is it not this very element of sin — not temptation, be it observed, but sin — which is constantly limiting us? Sin does not prevent sympathy, but it limits its power, kills the life out of it. When the blind undertakes to lead the blind, must they not both fall into the ditch?

But look at the other side of this truth. The more tempted, and at the same time the more sinless we are, the greater our capacity for true sympathetic power. The words of a good man knowing nothing of the temptations of the wine-cup might have but little effect upon the ine-briate, as compared with the words of one who had wrestled with and overcome the tempter, and thus knew the power of the demon that had his grip upon the soul of his brother man.

It is not enough, therefore, to declare that Christ shared our human experiences, and can be touched with a feeling of our infirmities. To this must be added the fact that He was tempted in all points like as we are, yet without sin. And this it is which makes His sympathy so full, so real, so powerful. For the love of His life, and the truth of His wisdom, flow down to us untrammelled and divine. And so the sympathy of Christ, when we understand it, is the loving presence and help of the Lord in His Divine Humanity; a sympathy, it is true, which we may be heedless of, or rudely reject, but which yearns on undiminished and undismayed.

Sympathy for childhood and its simple life; for His Humanity passed through the conditions of child-life. And the Gospels tell us that the Child of Nazareth submitted Himself to Mary and Joseph; and that " He increased in wisdom and stature, and in favor with God and man."

Sympathy for youth, with its perplexities and impetuous throbbing life ; just as years ago He looked into the earnest face of the rich young ruler who knelt at his feet, and "beholding him loved him."

Sympathy for honest work; for the life of the Son of Man was one of natural and spiritual toil; and none could say more touchingly or truly, "I am among you as one that serveth."

Sympathy in temptation; for the Humanity of our blessed Lord was assailed at every point; and He met the tempter face to face, and felt his power, and drove him back, saying, "Get thee behind Me, Satan!"

Sympathy with sorrow; for "He bore our griefs and carried our sorrows," and was Himself "a man of sorrows and acquainted with grief."

Sympathy in death. Mocked, buffeted, and spit upon, the Son of Man did not refuse to walk through the valley of the shadow of death. So He let His enemies lead Him to Calvary; let them watch and taunt Him in His last hours. "And He made His grave with the wicked, and with the rich in His death; because He had done no violence, neither was any deceit in His mouth." But He arose from the dead, and ascended into heaven, the Resurrection and the Life for all the world, saying to every dying soul, "I am He that liveth and was dead; and behold, I am alive forevermore, Amen; and have the keys of hell and of death."

And so, in whatever way we look, the Divine Humanity of Jesus Christ is seen to be in communion with our world and life, until we grow to feel that He makes our humanities His care, and feels for us, and sympathizes with us, — He, the great Refuge, the Divine Friend, standing among us and saying, as He said years ago, "Come unto Me, all ye that labor and are heavy laden, and I will give you rest. Take my yoke upon you, and learn of Me: for I am meek and lowly in heart; and ye shall find rest unto your souls."

THE TEMPTATIONS OF CHRIST.

Oh, who is this of lowly mien,
  Dear Son of Man! — tempted yet pure,
  Who buildeth love's foundation sure
In human hearts where sin had been?
    'T is Christ the Nazarene!

Oh, who is this with wounded side,
  With crimsoned brow and nail-pierced hands,
  Before whose death-bowed head fierce bands
Of dusky foes flee terrified?
    'T is Christ the Crucified!

Oh, who is this in garb of war,
  Dyed with the red of victory
  O'er hosts of sin and misery,
Whose hand alone strife's burden bore?
    'T is Christ the Conqueror!

                                        C. S.
Written for this volume.

V.

Ꮓhe Ꮓemptations of Ꮓhrist.

✠

*" Who is this that cometh from Edom, with dyed gar-
ments from Bozrah ? this that is glorious in His apparel,
travelling in the greatness of His strength ? "*

" I that speak in righteousness, mighty to save."

*" Wherefore art Thou red in Thine apparel, and Thy
garments like him that treadeth in the wine-vat ? "*

*" I have trodden the wine-press alone ; and of the people
there was none with Me. . . . And I looked and there was
none to help; and I wondered that there was none to
uphold."*

✠

E VERY one must feel that the bare recital of
incidents in any life falls very far short
of revealing that life. Without some knowledge
of the underlying motives and struggles, without
some idea of the hopes and doubts, the joys and
sorrows that have combined and recombined
within those incidents, we make but poor work

of our biographies. Can we doubt this, — that
lives are rich and great just in proportion as their
experiences are deep and spiritual ?

We turn to the great figures of the Gospels,
and find them all to be human like ourselves :
beings with passions, which, on a sudden, can
fire the loving breast of John and drive him
to the verge of invoking lightning to shatter the
inhospitable dwellings of the Samaritans; with
fears which turn the man of stone into a quick-
sand of deceit; with doubts which wither the
faith of a Thomas, until it seems to lie only in his
finger-tips. We find all tempted, and but one
sinless figure among them. And if this seems
strange, then we need to correct our ideas of the
religious life, and instead of thinking of it as a
tame, colorless existence, — a kind of passionless,
nerveless thing, which should be dead alike to the
pleasures and pains of this world, — to think of
it as a life roused to a pitch of feeling, capable of
a degree of temptation and remorse, restless for
a time with great anxious thoughts such as a
merely natural life could not experience. In a

word, a life with Christ opens man's inner spirit-
nature, and into it rush mighty influences which
penetrate wide and deep, and bring out widely
opposite possibilities of good and evil. And we
cannot justly compare such a life, which has been
deepened, expanded, purified by repentance, with
one which, though it should be outwardly correct
and agreeable, has never got beyond its morality,
never lost itself in the intricacies and solemnities
of a life with God, having lived contentedly on
the outermost rim of its humanity.

Look at the life of Christ. The prophet, in
spiritual description of Him, says, " He was
a man of sorrows, and acquainted with grief."
Yet we do not understand these words to mean
that outwardly our Lord's life was a sad or
dejected one. There were times, indeed, when
He did not conceal His sorrow. But there is
abundant evidence in the Gospels that for the
most part the life which men saw Him living
was serene; that it did not seem distressed and
cast down like ours. He did not come with the
cold austerity of the desert preacher, but entered

with such kindly companionship into the life of
the men about Him, that the strict religionists
of the day pointed their scornful fingers at Him,
and said, "Behold, a gluttonous man, and a
wine-bibber; a friend of publicans and sinners."
He travelled the white, dusty roads, going afoot
from village to village; He entered the boats of
the fishermen, and taught the curious listeners
that stood at the lake's edge; He would sit on
the grassy slope of some mountain, with the flowers about Him, and tell the people of a Providence more tender of their spiritual growth than
of the blooming lilies; He went in and out of the
homes of the people, healing all manner of sickness and all manner of disease, soothing many a
smarting spirit with the balm of His love.   And
yet, if we were to put together all the incidents of
His life, — the things, that is, which men saw, —
would that reveal the Saviour Christ?   Could we,
from a mere knowledge of such incidents, know
Him ?

When His earthly ministry drew to a close,
on the night of the last supper, looking into

the anxious faces of the little company around Him, He summed up His life and their ministry in these significant words : " Ye are they which have continued with Me in My temptations." How touching, how stirring, and yet how unexpected these words are ! " Ye are they which have continued with Me in My temptations." He does not say, " Ye are they whom I called from the shores of Galilee ; " or, " Ye are they who have witnessed My miracles and heard My teachings ; " but, " Ye are they which have continued with Me in My *temptations.*" Let us note carefully that in saying this the Lord is summarizing the experiences of His life. He is not looking back to some one dread experience, such as the temptation in the wilderness. He is looking over His entire ministry, and pointing out a class of experiences which have " continued " throughout that ministry. Viewed in this way, these words are most remarkable. They give us an important clew to His real inner life.

Now, in studying the temptations of Christ we

need to have a true idea of temptation itself. To many, temptation means simply an allurement to do wrong. Evil presents itself in an attractive form, and the enticement is called a temptation. And while it is not denied that this is one form of temptation, still the temptation-combats which no really Christian man ever yet escaped need a fuller classification. Granted that in its early development the Humanity of Christ was not exempt from even this kind of temptation, — for His experiences included all of ours, from the simplest to the subtlest, — still, is it conceivable that He was involved in one life-long struggle to withstand the common allurements of the world and of the flesh ? Let us not shrink from the Lord's statement that He was tempted, and tempted continually. But if we make this fact to mean that He was never free from the gross, the cheap enticements to wrong which affect us, we inevitably degrade those struggles, and rob them of their chief solemnity. Because of this gross conception, many shrink from contemplating the temptations of their Saviour. It pains them to

think about them. It troubles them to understand them.

Furthermore, many instinctively associate sin
with temptation; and this only adds to their
perplexity. They seem to feel that temptation
is a mark of evil. The really pure man, to them,
is unassailable. But this, too, is a fallacy, and,
in the light of Christ's experiences, a serious
fallacy. There is no virtue in being untempted.
The vessel that sails away, and spreads her great
white wings to favorable winds, and is borne
smoothly and swiftly on prosperous currents, is
no better than one that has to sail close-hauled,
and goes plunging and staggering through the
storm, masts and cordage strained near to snap-
ping, waves breaking over her, and every man
on board doing his utmost to keep her afloat.
The storms come, be sure of that! God's way
is in the sea, and His path in many waters. And
we have taken a pitifully poor view of the Christian life, if we look at it as a means of escaping
those great soul-struggles which, say what one
will, require the highest courage, and put the

thews and sinews of the spirit to the severest test. Temptation, bravely resisted, does not mar a man. It is no sign of sinfulness.

And so, when Christ says He was tempted continually, that does not take away from the greatness or the sanctity of His nature. Nay, when we remember that He was tempted and was yet sinless, do we not involuntarily draw nearer to Him, that in learning of His struggles, something of strength and consolation may flow down to us?

What can we say of those temptations? The subject is not a difficult one, if certain facts are understood. Man is subject to influences from both the heavenly and the infernal worlds. Between the two his spirit often falters. He inherits, as we all must see, a nature which is full, not of sins, but of tendencies to sin. And the struggle which ensues when he is assailed, and his evil proclivities aroused, — the struggle, the wrestle, with its moments of fearful uncertainty, — this we call temptation.

At first these struggles are of a simple nature.

The evils aroused are of a gross, almost material kind, and hence are more easily seen and grappled with. But if the spiritual life advances, these struggles become of a more interior character, and are harder to control. And the farther one advances, the more subtle are the attacks made upon his life. They take less and less tangible shapes, and become known to him, oftentimes, only through a certain sense of desolation and misery, prompting the spirit to doubt and despair.

Apply this to Christ. He took upon Himself a human nature like our own. It was more than a physical body. It was a nature with a capacity to think and feel and suffer as we do; the difference being, that we have a created, finite soul, whereas Christ's Humanity had the one uncreated, infinite soul. But because the nature He took on was human, it was approachable, like ours, by evil. And the Gospels say that these assaults upon His Humanity were continual. Moreover, they grew in interior intensity.

We do not attempt to define them in their

subtlest forms. There were pains of spirit which we can never know. None but the keenest anguish could have brought the bloody sweat upon His brow. But there are some things which we may partly understand, and by them gain a somewhat clear idea of the temptations which the Son of Man endured. These we would study.

The Lord, when He entered upon His public ministry, came forth in the full consciousness of His divine power. He knew, as He afterwards said, that He had the power to lay down His life, and the power to take it again. He knew, before He entered Cana of Galilee, that He could turn water into wine. He knew, moreover, that He had power on earth to forgive sins; that He was man's great deliverer, man's eternal Lord and Master. "Ye call Me Master, and Lord; and ye say well, for so I am." There is no shrinking from this supreme position. But this very consciousness of power and divinity was exposed to the self-love of the whole human race, and to the love of dominion of all the infernal worlds.

To what temptations would this subject Him?

There would be the temptation to compel human allegiance, to force the understanding to know Him and the heart to love Him. For the Saviour yearned to be known and received, that He might give men of His joy and make their joy full. How sweet the prayer at the close of His ministry: "Holy Father, keep through Thine own name those whom Thou hast given Me. . . . While I was with them in the world, I kept them in Thy name: those that Thou gavest Me I have kept." It gives us but a glimpse of the joy our Saviour had felt during those three years in keeping these men within the sphere of His love. Then we turn to the world, and find how blind and unresponsive it had been. He had come unto His own, but His own received Him not. The children of Jerusalem would not come under the wings of His mercy. They misunderstood Him, they maligned Him, they injured Him. Ah! from what a mighty depth of sorrow must that touching cry have risen, "The Son of Man hath not where to lay His head!" It was at men's souls that He was knocking; and the

human heart was the pillow on which He longed
to lay His head.

And do we think He was never tempted to
break down those bolted doors and compel His
people to receive Him? Yet we know that to
the very last moment He left men free. He
fairly pleads with the world, and says, "Take My
yoke upon you, and learn of Me: for I am meek
and lowly in heart; and ye shall find rest unto
your souls;" but He is true to the prophecy
which had said of Him, "He shall not strive nor
cry, neither shall any man hear His voice in the
streets." He will be the Good Shepherd: always
leading, never driving; calling the sheep by name,
but not injuring them with stones.

Perhaps there is another side to this, which
we should not be afraid to examine. The Lord
was not only conscious of His power, but conscious also of His absolute purity. He knew
that silence must be the only answer of His bitter-
est enemies when He asked, "Which of you con-
vinceth Me of sin?" He knew that He was
the very Truth itself. He knew that He was

laying down His life for the world, from the deepest and tenderest love. "In His love and in His pity He redeemed them." Yet think how the world requited Him! how it blasphemed Him! how it scourged Him! how it killed Him! He knew the enormity of the sin. Did the spirits of evil never torture Him with suggestions to avenge, to condemn? Was He not driving them off from His worn and suffering Humanity, when, as the cross was slowly lifted, He prayed, "Father, forgive them, for they know not what they do"?

And then, there was the temptation to vindicate Himself; to answer every false accusation; to resist by argument every denial. Do we not know what it is to be spoken against falsely? Do we not know what it is, not simply to be misunderstood, but misrepresented; to have our aims misjudged; to have evil motives attributed when we feel we are innocent? And do we not know, too, what an effort is required to keep silent at such times; or if not to remain wholly silent, to answer in the spirit of peace and love?

But who was ever maligned as our Lord was? When brought to trial, false witnesses were suborned to swear to some guilt. But He was dumb with silence; He held his peace even from good; it was only His sorrow that was stirred. He bore with silence the coarse witticisms of Herod and his soldiery. Twice He was brought before Pilate, stood face to face with His accusers; but He let them demand His life, for He had long since given it to them.

"He was brought as a lamb to the slaughter; and as a sheep before her shearers is dumb, so He opened not His mouth."

One other form of temptation the Lord had to endure. From the moment He began His ministry, He knew to what it would lead. He saw the hill of Calvary long before He ascended it. Several times He pointed it out to His disciples. Shortly before the dread scenes were enacted, He told them how "He must go unto Jerusalem, and suffer many things of the elders, and chief priests, and scribes, and be killed, and be raised again the third day." One loving man stood listening there, who could not bear to think of such sufferings coming to His Master; and he cried out at once, "Be it far from Thee, Lord; this shall not be unto Thee." But the Lord turned to Peter and said, "Get thee behind Me, Satan; thou art a stumbling-block unto Me." "Satan!" "stumbling-block!" How plainly these words reveal the temptation put in His way by this honest man's love. "Shall we smite with the sword?" the little band whispered eagerly when the mob came out against Him. And before an answer can be given, Peter has rushed upon the servant of the high priest. But Jesus rebuked His champion; and He said, "Thinkest thou that I cannot now pray to My Father, and He shall presently give Me more than twelve legions of angels? But how, then, shall the Scriptures be fulfilled, that thus it must be?" The temptation fell from Him; He would not refuse to drink the cup.

And this brings us to consider the direst temptation of all, — the Passion of the Cross.

Three years of loving work among all classes of

men have passed away; and now the Redeemer
of all souls has come up to Jerusalem for the last
time. For the last time He has tasted of the
fruit of the vine, until it shall be drunk in new-
ness in the kingdom of heaven. The meal is
over. The last admonitions to the little company
have ended in prayer for their spiritual safety and
consecration. The men, with their Master, have
sung the great Messianic Psalm. And now they
pass out into the night. They go through the
eastern gate, then down a steep path, then over
the brook Kedron, into a garden guarded to-day
by "eight aged and gnarled olive-trees, upon
which the suns of many centuries have risen and
set."

"Into the woods my Master went,
    Clean forspent, forspent.
Into the woods my Master came,
    Forspent with love and shame.
But the olives they were not blind to Him,
The little gray leaves were kind to Him:
The thorn-tree had a mind to Him,
    When into the woods He came.

"Out of the woods my Master went,
    And He was well content.

Out of the woods my Master came,
Content with death and shame.
When Death and Shame would woo Him last,
From under the trees they drew Him last:
'T was on a tree they slew Him — last,
When out of the woods He came."

We do not attempt to draw the scene of the
Passion. Men saw the evidences of suffering, indeed, not the deepest causes of it. Can we hear
Christ say to His disciples, "Fear not them
which kill the body," and then feel that it was
the knowledge of approaching death that forced
the cry, "If it be possible, let this cup pass from
Me!" We dare not say there were no physical
pains; but this we may know: death had no ter-
rors for the Resurrection and the Life. Beyond
the heights of Calvary, He could look into the
serene vistas of the higher world. Men might
mock Him, scourge Him, nail Him to a tree; He
would not resist them, for had He not come to
lay down His life for their sakes? And do we,
in thought, gather about His cross, pitying His
pains as though they were only of the body, and as
if it were so hard for the Humanity to die? Why,

that is what the priests and elders thought! That
is what the gaping multitude thought! and it
only made their triumph seem the greater. But
Christ said never a word about bodily pain and
fear. He took Peter, James, and John into the
inner recess of the garden, and told them the secret of it all when He said, " My *soul* is exceeding sorrowful, even unto death." All through
life, as we have seen, the Humanity of our Lord
had been assaulted. Every form of evil or falsity
which can invade a human nature, He met and
put down. Their multitude is pointed out in
those prophetic words : " They are more than the
hairs of mine head." Then came the final on-
slaught ; the one last desperate effort of infuriated
spirits to break through His Humanity and
make it captive.

There was a suffering greater than physical,
however torturing that may have been, — pains
striking deeper than the flesh. And when our
Saviour cries, " My God, My God, why hast Thou
forsaken Me ! " we may know that the Humanity
is being wrung with keenest spiritual agonies,

and that the life which had long continued in temptation-combats is closing in one final, decisive, appalling struggle.

And what was accomplished by these spiritual struggles? First, they were the means by which everything earth-born was put away and the Humanity made divine. According to this law we ourselves are regenerated. For just in proportion as we triumph over evil, good takes its place. The other result was the subjugation of the infernal worlds, and man's consequent redemption; that is, his restoration to spiritual freedom.

To any one accepting the Gospels, there can be no doubt that the Saviour came in conflict with the spirits of evil. It was one of the first things which the people did, when the Lord's fame began to spread abroad, to bring those who were possessed with devils. What a revelation of man's condition! For the Gospels speak of it as quite a common thing. And two facts we notice in the Saviour's contact with demoniacs, — the devils always knew Him; the devils always feared Him.

They knew Him far better, oftentimes, than
the men and women about Him. And why?
and how? Evidently because by His divine
presence He was effecting a judgment or separation among them, and interposing Himself between them and the human beings they would
have enslaved. " Let us alone," cried one of
them ; " what have we to do with Thee, Thou
Jesus of Nazareth? Art Thou come to destroy
us? I know Thee who Thou art, the Holy One
of God." He was teaching in the synagogue
at Capernaum, when suddenly the demoniac fell
writhing and howling at the Saviour's feet. We
can imagine the men and women springing to
their feet in a panic of excitement and fear; and
He, the new, the ridiculed Teacher, the one calm
figure among them! " Hold thy peace, and come
out of him," He simply says. And with one
final struggle, one last shout of anger and of pain,
the unclean spirit is gone. There lies the man,
released from his awful bondage. That, surely,
was his redemption, his restoration to spiritual
freedom through the power of the Redeemer.

And what the Lord did for that man He did for the whole human race. Only, in this and some other instances the work was visible. He let men see what He was doing for them spiritually. He let them into this large secret of His ministry; namely, that He was remanding the spirits of darkness to their own abodes, and breaking up a tyranny which they had acquired through man's sinfulness. For men were in bondage, and He told them so. And He told them that He was their deliverer, — ay, that He was the One whom their Scriptures had long foretold would come " to proclaim liberty to the captives, and the opening of the prison to the bound." So He let evil assault Him, that He might overcome its tyranny and lead captivity captive. In this consists our redemption. " Let the redeemed say so, whom He hath redeemed from the hand of the enemy."

We consider one point more. It may be asked, " How could temptation cause the Son of Man a moment's anguish, if, as is maintained throughout these pages, His inmost soul was

Divinity itself? Could not evil be driven away like so much chaff, which a breath of wind will scatter? But we are to remember that the assaults were made upon the Humanity, and that it lay with the Humanity to yield or to turn to the Divinity within, and meet evil with a holy strength. The Humanity felt the assaults; and had it not been unfailingly true to its divine nature, might in some moment have proved as frail as we are. There is always the possibility with us to lay hold, as it were, of the divine nature the instant evil assails us, and meet it with ample strength. But no! we either succumb at once, or else we rely upon ourselves; and so we suffer defeat again and again. But this is precisely what the Humanity of Christ did not do. And its perfection consisted in its unvarying fidelity to the divine nature within. It was stormed and assaulted, and with what bitterness we shall never know. As with a man, it seemed to struggle alone. But always it conquered, — conquered by using, as of itself, the powers of the divine Fatherhood within.

What lessons come down to us from those great trial-hours of Christ! And what rebukes! Think of it! Nothing that evil could devise, that He did not meet and put down! Tempted at all points, but without sin! So calm and gentle in His outward bearing! So true, so enduring in struggles men could not see! And we are tempted, too, — tempted, and we often fall; tempted, and we sometimes triumph. And when we triumph, it is through the conquering power of Christ, who suffered and overcame that He might give us the strength to suffer and overcome. For, in the language of the apostle, "In that He Himself hath suffered being tempted, He is able to succor them that are tempted." Ay, for this is what He said: "Be of good cheer: I have overcome the world."

THE SANCTITY OF CHRIST.

Come, my Way, my Truth, my Life!
Such a Way, as gives us breath;
Such a Truth, as ends all strife;
Such a Life, as killeth death.

Come, my Light, my Feast, my Strength!
Such a Light, as shows a feast;
Such a Feast, as mends in length;
Such a Strength, as makes his guest.

Come, my Joy, my Love, my Heart!
Such a Joy, as none can move;
Such a Love, as none can part;
Such a Heart, as joys in love.

Herbert.

VI.

The Sanctity of Christ.

✠

"For their sakes I sanctify Myself, that they also might be sanctified."

✠

THE sanctity of Christ is essential to Christianity; for Christianity is essentially the following of the Lord Jesus Christ. Differently from every other teacher, He places Himself before His teachings. It is not merely a new philosophy, or code of ethics that He brings: *it is Himself.* His claim is far greater than that He knows the truth and can therefore proclaim it. He is more than a teacher of it. He declares Himself to be the perfect embodiment of it. In short, He is the Truth, — the Word made flesh; the Truth living and breathing.

Now, every true teacher is presumably in the effort to come into correspondence with his teachings. But of whom, save the Lord Jesus Christ, could we say that the correspondence attained is so perfect and absolute as to entitle him to declare himself to be the truth? Socrates discourses beautifully of immortality. What if he had said to those gathered about him in his cell, "I am the Resurrection and the Life"![1]

And with this difference in the teacher comes a difference in method. The human teacher pleads for the truth as something apart from himself; he presents it as something vastly superior to himself. He could not justly say, "If you would know the truth, study me." He would say, rather: "Do not judge of the truth by what I am. Consider it apart from me. Judge of it as though I had not spoken it. The truth is superior to me. I am not that Light, but am come simply to bear witness of that Light. I am only a voice crying out in

[1] See Note C.

the wilderness, 'Make straight the way of the Lord.'"

But the Christ called upon men to believe first of all in Him. For proof of His divine claims, He bade men look at His life and works. "The works that I do in My Father's name," He said to those who were questioning His claims, "they bear witness of Me." "If I do not the works of My Father, believe Me not." To His apostles He appealed, "Believe Me for the very works' sake." From whatever class His followers came, they always came in answer to this one, simple summons, "Follow Me." Why does the Lord insist upon this personal devotion? Not, surely, that it may add to His glory, — that is already infinite, — but because without this personal element, religion becomes a cold, intellectual, almost hopeless thing. The Lord came to the world and taught it deep, searching truths. He stated the conditions of salvation and the elements of a heavenly character. It is rightly claimed that the Sermon on the Mount contains the rules of the highest possible morality and religion. But what

if the Saviour had simply appeared on that one
day and preached that sermon? What if we
knew nothing of Him who sat on the mountain
slope and said, "Blessed are the poor in spirit"!
Truth in the abstract! Cold rules telling us how
we should live! How long would Christianity
have lasted? What power of resistance would it
have had against persecution? How far beyond
a few schoolmen, who might have studied them
as they studied the philosophy of Plato, would
Christ's teachings have spread? Would the common people have flocked to the academies to learn
of this new religion? And if they had, would
they have been affected by it, or even understood
it, in its impersonal form? Was it not its personal quality which gave it such power, — the
life that had been lived for them; the sufferings
which had been endured for them; the death that
had included them? The truth became clear and
dear to them just so far as they saw it in Him.
And this was in accordance with the Saviour's
wish; for He had said, "Take My yoke upon
you, and learn of Me."

Since, then, Christ identifies Himself with the truth of His religion, and since this new religion consists primarily in the acceptance of Him, then the absolute sanctity of Christ is of vital importance. And by sanctity, as applied to Christ, we mean holiness. We mean especially the holiness of His Humanity: the descent of the Divine into the Human, — a process which was synchronous with the displacement of maternal inheritances through temptation-combats, and which constituted what He called His glorification. If this sanctity can be established, the Saviour stands upon a distinctly higher eminence than that attained by any teacher or reformer, however illustrious. If His sanctity cannot be maintained, the conclusion is obvious. Upon what grounds do we base our belief in the sanctity of the Lord Jesus Christ?

We notice, first of all, Christ's own testimony. And in doing this we need to remember that it is the testimony of One who set the highest value upon humility. He knew how inevitably self-exaltation ends in abasement; nor would He allow

the rich young ruler to call Him, out of mere
compliment, "good." He does not deny the
quality, for He announces Himself as "the Good
Shepherd." But those who call Him good must
do so knowing what it involves; "for none is
good, save One, that is God." He commends
repentance, and prefers the publican's cry of remorse to the smooth self-gratulation of the Pharisee. He invites the world to come to Him, not as
One who glories in His sanctity, but for the very
reason that He is "meek and lowly in heart."
The claim of sanctity, coming from the lips of
such an One, compels our thoughtfulness.

Let us observe Him in the presence of His
enemies on the night of His arrest. He is standing bound before the high priest. Although it
is midnight, the chief priests, scribes, and elders
have been summoned together by the news that
the Nazarene has been arrested and is now in
the high priest's palace. They needed no urging,
we may be sure, but hurried through the dark,
narrow streets to the palace, crossed the court-
yard where a number of servants and officers were

huddled about a fire, — poor, despairing Peter
among the rest, — then up a flight of steps to
the council chamber where sat the high priest
in his pontifical robes. Yes; it was no mistake.
There stands the Nazarene bound with cords and
guarded by officers. Taken at last! He who had
told them that the publicans and harlots would
go into the kingdom of God before them; who
had likened them to whitened sepulchres, is at
length in their power! Now He shall answer
for all He has said!

So Caiaphas asks Him about His disciples and
about His doctrine. And He answers him, "I
spake openly to the world; I ever taught in the
synagogue, and in the temple, whither the Jews
alway resort, and in secret have I said nothing.
Why askest thou Me? Ask them which heard
Me, what I have said unto them; behold, they
know what I said." His appeal is to the world.
He challenges it to bring forth a single accusation
against Him.

But here the proceedings are rudely interrupted;
for one of the officers turns angrily upon Him,

and in violation of all justice, decency, or man-
liness, strikes the bound Teacher a blow in the
face. And the despised and injured One turns
to the ruffian, and, still challenging disproofs of
His innocence, says with gentle dignity: "If I
have spoken evil, bear witness of the evil: but
if well, why smitest thou Me?"

Let us observe Him on another occasion. He
is in one of the temple courts. As usual, many
are about Him. He is telling His hearers of
their spiritual slavery, — a theme most unpopular
to a Jew, for a portion of his morning prayer ran
thus: "Blessed be the Lord our God, King of
the universe, who has made me a free man."[1]
He tells them that His Truth will make them
free. But they become incensed, dispute His
statements, and accuse Him of madness. But
He asks them one and all, "Which of you con-
vinceth Me of sin?"

That which appeals to us in both these incidents is Christ's plea of absolute sinlessness. He
has taught openly where all could hear Him;

[1] Quoted in Geikie's "Life and Words of Christ."

He has lived in plain sight of friends and foes; He has been watched; His enemies have tried to entrap Him in some evil word or deed; and yet He declares His sinlessness, and summons His very enemies as His witnesses. Pilate, who, to ease his troubled conscience, would gladly have found some defect in his prisoner, is compelled to say, "I find in Him no fault at all." Judas feels the money received for his Master's life like a millstone about his neck; and that which rives his heart is the knowledge that he has betrayed innocent blood. His crime turns black before him as he realizes that he has sinned against the sinless One.

And yet we realize how inadequately this word "sinless" expresses the truth of Christ's sanctity. It is too negative. It is nerveless and colorless. Not to be evil is one thing; to be genuinely and positively righteous is quite another thing. Now, Christ's life was of all things supremely positive. Let any one put into His mouth such utterances as these: "I am not selfish," "I am not worldly," "I am not evil," and we feel at once that the whole conception of Christ is changed, if not destroyed. But instead, what do we find? The one truly positive life. Sinless? Yes. Blameless? Yes. Not, however, by mere self-repression, but by absolute holiness.

We cannot open a single page of our Gospels without meeting this positive element. How does He meet the sneer of His enemies, "Thou art not yet fifty years old, and hast Thou seen Abraham?" This is what He says: "Verily, verily I say unto you, before Abraham was, I am." He claims the title of the God of their fathers, — the great "I AM." In the consciousness of His inner divine nature He proclaims Himself the Being of the universe, — not an eternal "I am not," but "I AM" — infinite, positive life and essence. "I *am* the Way, the Truth, and the Life." "I *am* the Light of the world." "I *am* the Good Shepherd." "I *am* the Vine." "I *am* the Bread of Life." "I *am* the Resurrection and the Life."

Here is a display of positive being! a certainty of character, an absoluteness of goodness and truth, which the world, if it would, cannot shake off. And this, too, in One who said, " I am meek and lowly in heart." Ah! what a rebuke to our natural judgments! We admire the man who, as we say, has a will of his own; a man who has something of the " Boanerges " about him; who, instead of being meek and lowly, is at times a "son of thunder; " a man who can not only take, but give, a powerful blow; and we pity, perhaps, the meek and the lowly, the poor in spirit, and the peacemakers, out of a feeling that there is in such Christ-like qualities a lack of positiveness and strength. But the meek and the lowly One stands before us,—stands before us and confounds us with His perfect strength. In His gentleness, He will take the little children in His arms and bless them. In His tenderness, He will try to hush the wails of the women as He slowly makes His way to the crucifixion. He will pray for His executioners as they drive the nails through His quivering flesh. "Meek and lowly," indeed! But there is an unconquerable strength in that meekness, and an eternal majesty in that lowliness !

From verbal testimony, let us turn to the life itself. And the more deeply we look into that life, the more clearly shall we see its absolute perfection. Those very years in Nazareth, concerning which the Gospels tell us so little, proclaim His sanctity with silent eloquence. For they tell of complete self-abnegation and self-control, such as belong only to a nature supremely perfect. We have already seen that the Humanity of Christ was related to the Divine within Him as our earthly nature is related to our inmost nature, or soul. Of this relation He was conscious. He knew what power was His. He understood His mission. He longed to set men spiritually free. And yet there is no impatience. He makes no display of His divinity. He does not startle the people of the village with claims of His omnipotence. He does not assert His divine superiority over them. On the contrary, He accommodates Himself to their conditions. The greatest of all becomes the servant of all, — a carpenter in their little village; building them their homes; making each day a day of lowly service; living so simply among them, that at the end of thirty years the people of the village — those even who had lived under the same roof and passed as His kinsmen — know Him only as the carpenter. Remembering always who He was ; remembering that, as He said, He was in the Father, and the Father in Him, how wonderful are these quiet years of toil ! What testimony they furnish to the perfect sanctity of His nature ! For who but one supremely true and holy would be capable of such patience, condescension, and self-denial ?

How plainly this sanctity appears all through the Saviour's public ministry ! He is so calm, so enduring ! The people's heart was indeed waxed gross, and their ears were dull of hearing, and their eyes they had closed. Even His apostles were " slow of heart." And yet He taught them so patiently ! He clothed the truth for them in the simplest forms, relating to them parables of the Shepherd and the sheep, of the Sower and the seed, of the Vine and the branches. His enemies laid snares for Him; the spirits of evil assailed Him ; His followers misunderstood

Him; one of them betrayed Him! Yet still
He went calmly on; not without pain, but always without bitterness. There is no dread, as
with men, lest His plans shall fail. He knew the
end, and saw that it was only by the complete
sacrifice of His Humanity that the work of redemption could be wrought. He strengthened
His Humanity by bringing it into communion
with the divine Fatherhood of His nature, saying,
as none of us have ever said, " Thy will be done ; "
then went calmly forth, — went forth to spiritual
conflicts too fearful for us to know; went forth
to trial and to death.

His sanctity appears in the gentle dignity with
which He bore ill-treatment. What so fully
tests character as self-control under unjust and
cruel treatment? What more trying than to
have one's holiest aims misjudged; to be accused
or suspected of wrong where no wrong is; to
have good requited by evil? Possessing all
power in heaven and in earth, He never once
availed Himself of His omnipotence to punish
His worst enemies. He never harmed a single

creature. Sin was hateful in His eyes, but the
sinner was an object of His compassion. He
fairly mourns over Judas. The man's perfidy
fills Him with anguish. It is on His heart as
He sits down with the twelve to that last Passover meal. He might have arraigned His betrayer; He might have exposed his treachery.
Their hands meet as each dips his morsel of
bread in the *charoseth.* "What thou doest, do
quickly." There is no anger in the words. Soon
they meet again, and in a spot which, it would
seem, was hallowed by many tender associations.
It is an awful moment in the life of Iscariot.
And how is he met? The kiss is not refused;
but oh, what blow could have caused such pain!
"Judas, betrayest thou the Son of Man with a
kiss?" Love — wounded, ill-requited love —
speaking in accents of profound pity while the
darkness is gathering around them both, still merciful, still free of bitterness, held out to the man in
these parting words of sorrow!

> "Judas, dost thou betray Me with a kiss?
> Canst thou find hell about My lips, and miss
> Of life just at the gates of life and bliss?"

We come away from such a scene with the feeling that one who could bear evil in the spirit in which the Saviour bore it was indeed perfect and divine.

One test of a true life the Lord gave to His apostles, to which He Himself submitted, — " Greater love hath no man than this, that a man lay down his life for his friends." The test involves more than a willingness to yield up one's physical life for the good of others. There is a daily laying down of the life — the abasement of selfish desires, the subordination of the earthly to the heavenly — which requires the highest heroism. The Lord made self-denial, of which the cross is the eternal emblem, a condition of the Christian life. " If any man will come after Me, let him deny himself, and take up his cross daily, and follow Me. For whosoever will save his life, shall lose it ; and whosoever will lose his life for My sake, the same shall save it."

How fully the Lord fulfilled this law of self-sacrifice ! " I lay down My life for the sheep," He said. None ever gave his life so willingly, so

universally, as the Son of Man. His very sanctity He declares to be won for the world's sake.
" For their sakes I sanctify Myself, that they also
might be sanctified through the truth." There
are no words more loving than these. " For
their sakes ! " Have we thought of the Lord's
glorification as being for His sake alone ? Then
we need to correct the thought. It is for our
sakes ; that He may bring a new power to bear
on our calloused souls, and sanctify us, raising us
up from death unto life. Is He tempted ? Ay,
truly, that overcoming the assaults of evil He
may be a ready and an all-powerful help when we
are grappled. Is He mocked, and scourged, and
crucified ? Oh, we know the truth of it ; and by
the sufferings borne, and the victories won, He
comes to champion us to-day in our desperate
cause. Is He retiring to some lonely mountain
for the night ? Is He entering the shadows of
Gethsemane ? Is He, faint and bleeding, going
on to Calvary ? Then, remember He takes the
path for us, — for us, cold, sluggish, coward-
men, who read about those struggles, and try to

analyze them, and — God forgive us ! — even criticise them, yet will not place our cross upon our backs and follow daily in the path He trod !

"For their sakes I sanctify Myself." In these few words is revealed a truth which we would never forget, — that the sanctity of the Saviour came, as sanctity must ever come, through self-denial and spiritual conflict. We may say with reverence that His perfection cost Him days and years of struggle ; for it was attained by the displacement of everything in the Humanity which was not in exact correspondence with the Divine within. And this was only accomplished through a certain self-immolation, which He indicated whenever He spoke of laying down His life. The work of sanctification went on from day to day. There was a daily struggle with every least inheritance of that nature, woman-born. There was a daily combat with evil powers who would fain have beaten through those walls of life. There was a sweet and daily laying down of His natural life, bringing the Human and the Divine into closer and closer conjunction.

Of this spiritual self-sacrifice, few who saw Him could have had any true realization. Not even the apostles — those who, He said, had followed Him in the regeneration — understood this truth in its fulness. They could hear Him say, " The hour is come that the Son of Man should be glorified." They could hear His prayer, " And now, O Father, glorify Me with Thine own self." But did they know the solemn truth conveyed in these words ? Did they know that the Humanity and the Divinity of their Saviour had been so united that the Humanity itself was divine ? The power of His life they felt; they were drawn towards Him; the love and truth of His divinely-human nature lifted them upon a higher plane of life. And this same holy, uplifting influence was felt by many others, and has continued among Christians ever since.

In this fact — the sanctifying power of Christ — we find our highest proof of His sanctity. Something passes into the man who faithfully follows the Master, which elevates and enlarges his entire manhood. The man moves amid scenes

and industries which are common to all; yet
slowly, quite imperceptibly oftentimes to himself,
something of calmness, of patience, of strength,
of mercy, of self-denial, grows up within him,
and in a sense separates him from the world.
A new spirit pervades his life; new hopes, new
motives thrill it. Something, which cannot be
explained away, purifies and expands it. The
spirit of the Lord sanctifies it. And by this we
may know that He Himself is perfect and divine,
and that His religion is unfailingly true.

What, in all that we know of life, is more wonderful than this experience of salvation? To be
reclaimed from the world; to be turned from sinfulness; to have the Saviour come to a man's
heart, and, in the spirit of loving mercy, lay His
omnipotent hand upon our diseased frames, saying, "Be thou clean!" Now, as years ago, virtue goes out of Him. No wonder the multitudes
sought to touch Him! He was so true and holy,
and they so full of misery! To the early Christians this life was the most real, the most precious
thing their minds could possess. Why should it

be less to us, who are still summoned to follow in the footsteps of that life, and to enter heaven through that same sacred Door ? Why should it be less to us, who are beset with difficulties, and assaulted with temptations, and tormented by the lusts of the world and the burning of selfishness ? Why should it be less to us, who toil, and become weary and heavy-laden, and suffer pains of heart and of conscience which cast us down, and endure losses, and part with our friends and our loved ones in death ?

We are born into the world with souls unsanctified, and with strong proclivities to evil. Though each should think that he, at least, may escape experiences which have put the strength and patience of others to the test, yet sooner or later he lives to see his endurance tried. And as life brings out the inherited qualities of his nature, he feels more and more keenly the truth of the perfect One when he said, " Ye must be born again." Cares come, disappointments come, sorrows come ; come, too, the temptations which show a man the foes in his own breast, and involve him in such bitter strifes. And then, with some, will come the longing for a Sanctifier,— some one to give them the power to make their life a truer, sweeter thing than it is; some one to help lift it out of its selfishness. That feeling, when it first becomes distinctly felt, marks a crisis in our life. It is the brooding spirit of the Lord ruffling the face of the deep, putting motion into what was still and dead. We may, in our perversity, though sometimes in our ignorance, try many human physicians. We may try first this, then that scheme of improvement, only to find ourselves made nothing better, but rather worse. But the time may also come when, in our extremity, we shall go in simple faith to Jesus Christ; touch, as it were, with trembling fingers His blessed Person; and in that contact between our human and His divine life feel a power which heals and sanctifies.

"For their sakes I sanctify Myself, that they also might be sanctified." There is something intensely solemn in this fact of Christ's absolute perfection. We see so much that is imperfect, so

much that is sinful and weak in human nature, so
many mistakes and failures. What tears of peni-
tence ought we to have shed! What cries of remorse should have come from our lips! "God
be merciful to me a sinner!" is the heart-cry of
many a man. And then we turn to the divinely-
human life of the Son of Man, and find One who
could go through this world's experiences, beset
with difficulties and dangers, assailed by evil,
wronged, scorned, betrayed, a stranger in the
world, so little understood that as He stood with
the multitudes about Him He seemed alone, —
alone in the crowd, alone by the very divineness
of His life, — work to perform such as no man
could accomplish, experiences to undergo so deep
and intense that they would have withered the
strongest of us, — we find all this, and with it
this fact, this awful fact, of sinlessness, not one
least blemish! and we so easily discouraged, so
weak in temptation, so faithless and unbelieving.

Still before the world stands our blessed Lord
and Saviour. Still His hands are over us in
benediction. And still men are reaching out their

imploring hands to Him, like Jairus praying for his child, like Peter sinking amid the waves of Galilee, like the leper crying out in his misery, " Lord, if Thou wilt, Thou canst make me clean." He is the world's one sinless figure. He is its one perfect life. The world, with its sick and its sinful, lies at His feet; and He says through His Word, " Look unto Me and be ye saved, all the ends of the earth; for I am God, and there is none else."

THE MAJESTY OF CHRIST.

I brought my Lord unto a beetling hill,
To cast Him down:
He turned and looked on me — so calm, so still,
Without a frown —
I was o'erthrown.

I led against Him men in fierce array,
Him to enthrall:
He strove not; "I am He," I heard Him say:
They fear, and all
Before Him fall.

Alas! I would not own Him for my Lord;
I Him denied!
But then I met His gaze; He spoke no word;
With humbled pride,
I turned and cried.

Oh, may I ne'er forget His wondrous grace,
But ever cling
To Him, my Lord; let nought His reign displace,
But love e'er bring
To Christ my King!

C. S.

Written for this volume.

VII.

The Majesty of Christ.

✠

" Art Thou a King then ? "
" Thou sayest that I am a King."

✠

CHRIST'S entry into Jerusalem is the one incident during His ministry wherein He seemed to receive the glory due unto His name; the one occasion when He accepted the outward honors belonging to a king.

It was many a day since Jerusalem had seen such sights. The city was crowded with people coming from all parts of the country to the Passover. They usually travelled in companies, chanting the Psalms of David as they went. They crowded into the capital by the hundred thousand. Private houses became public; tents were pitched in the streets and outside the city.

The festival was always a stirring one; but this time there was an additional cause of excitement. The chief priests and Pharisees had given a commandment, that if any man knew where Christ was, he should show it, that they might take Him. And the men, meeting each other in the temple courts, or on the streets, or in their shops, would ask, "What think ye, that He will not come to the feast?" The city was on the *qui vive.* Should He come, a collision seemed inevitable; for the church authorities were determined to have Him apprehended, while, on the other hand, He was known to have many friends among the common people, especially the Galileans.

We may imagine, then, that there was no small excitement when the news came that He had left Bethany and was actually on His way to the city, followed by a large company of friends. The people poured out of the city gates by thousands. They cross the Kedron, and take the road for Bethany. Yes, there they come, down the white, dusty road. And there is the Teacher of Nazareth, coming, as the rulers and prophets of old used to come, riding on an ass, and a colt the foal of an ass. The excitement runs high. Some carpet the road with their garments; others cut down palm-branches and strew them in the way; while all send up shout after shout of welcome, and hail Him as King.

"Hosanna to the Son of David!" they cry. "Blessed is He that cometh in the name of the Lord!"

"Blessed be the kingdom of our father David, that cometh in the name of the Lord!"

"Blessed [they boldly cry] is the King of Israel, that cometh in the name of the Lord!"

"Peace in heaven, and glory in the highest!"

Down sweeps the procession, through the Kedron valley, over the brook, then up again to the city gate and into the streets of Jerusalem. Where are the chief priests and Pharisees now? Poor, baffled men! they are thoroughly dismayed. They see the excited multitudes, and whisper angrily to each other, "Behold, the world is gone after Him!" The tide of enthusiasm has rolled

11

from Galilee to Jerusalem. Some of them manage to make their way to the Messiah, and ask Him to rebuke His disciples. But He replies, "I tell you, that if these should hold their peace, the stones would immediately cry out."

And yet, who does not feel that these royal honors were not dear to our blessed Lord? For, after all, were they not the strongest testimony to how little the people really understood or cared for Him? What was temporal power or royal splendor to Him, who came to lay down His life for men's sake? He was indeed King, as all the angels know; nor did He ever reject the title. But His Kingship was much more royal than that of any Cæsar; and His kingdom was not of this world.

For once the Seer of Patmos beheld a great multitude, which no man could number, of all nations and kindreds and people and tongues, standing before the throne and before the Lamb, clothed with white robes, and palms in their hands. And he heard the chant of the angel choirs as it came rolling out of the opened heav-

ens : " Worthy is the Lamb that was slain, to
receive power, and riches, and wisdom, and
strength, and honor, and glory, and blessing ! "
This was royal welcome indeed ! For to those
purified spirits Christ was King, not of lands or
earthly principalities, but of their hearts. He
was their King, because His truth had won them
quite, and because they were happy in yielding
their souls to His regnant will.

But how different was the spirit of it all on
that day when the Saviour rode into Jerusalem
amid the hosannas of the multitude! The people were happy. For the moment they were
loyal. Why? Because the Saviour of souls was
there? No ! Because, as Luke declares in his
Gospel, " They thought that the kingdom of God
would immediately appear." The sudden re-
establishment of David's throne, in all its old-
time glory, — that was what they prayed for ; that
was what they expected. The kind Healer and
Uplifter of the human heart they had often
mocked, and would mock again. But let Him
come as their Messiah, — a monarch who would

crush the Roman yoke, which galled their proud
natures, and they would welcome Him indeed!
They would salute Him with palms! They would
spread their garments for Him! They would do
anything for Him if He would be Cæsar's Cæsar!
But when they found His Kingship meant truth,
and order, and purity in the heart, it took but
five days to turn their " Hosannas " into cries of
" Crucify Him ! "

And so, this entry into Jerusalem teaches us
two facts concerning the majesty of Christ :

He had the quality of majesty, otherwise He
would not have accepted these royal honors ;

But His majesty was not of a temporal
character.

He had the quality of majesty. We feel that
all through His ministry. We feel it even when
He is saying, " I am meek and lowly in heart."
We bow to it when He declares His homeless-
ness, and says so touchingly, " The Son of Man
hath not where to lay His head ! " We see it
when, for one moment, the veil is lifted and He
stands upon a mount in transfigured glory, his

face shining as the sun and His raiment white
and glistering.

We know nothing of the Redeemer's appearance. Whether, as some legends would have us
believe, His appearance was altogether unlovely,
in exact fulfilment of the prophecy, "He hath
no form, nor comeliness; and when we shall see
Him, there is no beauty that we should desire
Him;" or whether His was a majestic, beau-
teous presence, we know not. We do not need to
know. But this is not hidden from us, — there was
a certain power of life, issuing from His person,
which brought men to their knees time and again.

We cannot read our Gospels intelligently, if we
think of Christ only as a loving, docile, patient,
winning person. Our conception of Him is a
very weak one, if we leave out a certain spirit of
power and majesty to which the Gospels testify
again and again. Under every deed or utterance
of His there is a reserved, yes, a pent-up force,
which many felt and many feel. "He taught
them," say these precious records, "as one having
authority, and not as the Scribes." He legislates

beyond Moses and their fathers, with an eternal "I say unto you." And the people marvelled. Time and again they came to Him, the Gospels say, "worshipping," or "kneeling," or "falling at His feet," or "trembling and falling down to Him." He, without authority save that of the truth, could overturn the tables of the money-changers, and send their piles of coin spinning over the temple floor; drive out the sheep and oxen, and command that the great wicker cages full of doves should be taken hence. What wonder that the people should whisper to each other, "This is certainly the prophet!" or that some should go so far as to ask, "Is not this the Christ?"

See Him among the hills of Gadara. There is up there in some of those tombs which pierce the sides of the hill, a demoniac so wild and untamable that no one dares pass by that way. The people of the district had more than once pursued him, and caught him, and chained him, only to see the chains plucked asunder, and the fetters broken in pieces. But this morning a Galilean fishing-boat

has come to the shore. The Christ and His disciples step out. Instantly this wild, naked, fren-
zied man comes leaping down the mountain-side.
But while he is yet quite a distance off, the poor,
maddened thing falls cowering to the earth, and
with an awful cry exclaims, " What have I to do
with thee, Jesus, thou Son of the most high God?
Art Thou come hither to torment us before the
time?" The devil-legion in an agony of terror
through His gentle presence !

And what devils and satans felt, men felt too.
The people of Nazareth, at the end of that first
sermon He preached to them, rose up as one man,
seized Him, and led Him to the brow of the hill
whereon their city was built, with the intention of
casting Him down headlong. But, says the narrative, " He, passing through the midst of them,
went His way." In the bearing of the Son of
Man there must have been something so calm, so
pure, so true, that the angry men were awed by
it, lost their brutal courage, let go their hold, fell
back, and let Him pass unhurt in His simple
majesty through their broken ranks !

We see almost the same thing in Gethsemane.
Why should the mob be afraid of Jesus of Nazareth? They are armed with clubs and staves
and all manner of weapons : He has but a few
men about Him. Why, then, should they recoil
and fall to the ground when He advances to meet
them, and simply says "I am He"? With a
calmness and pureness and holy dignity, which
smote their coward consciences as not even a
flaming angel could have done, He stood there in
His simple majesty, and they dare not face Him!
Will any merely natural reasons suffice for these
things? Do they not tell of divine majesty and
power?

Now, we have the secret of it all in that memorable interview between Christ and the Roman
governor. Pilate, according to contemporary history, was an arbitrary, tyrannical ruler; by no
means adverse to the shedding of blood, and none
too scrupulous in the exercise of his authority, —
not at all the man to be awed by the quiet presence and a few calm words of a prisoner. Yet
the world knows how anxious he grew. We feel

that it is Pilate's trial; that the bound One is King, and the governor the subject. "Art Thou a King?" Pilate asks. No doubt there was contempt, humor, almost pity in the question; and so far from being serious, Pilate's thought was more, "Are you, bound, friendless, weary, sweet-minded man, a king? Have you a kingdom? Have you subjects?" And what we cannot forget is, that Christ affirmed His Kingship to this Roman, and told him the secret of His majesty in words which the world is just beginning to understand.

He was addressing an officer of that nation which was the splendid tyrant of the world, and the symbols of its idolatry and of its wealth were flashing out upon Him. Yet He turned to the man and said: "Thou sayest that I am a king [a form of assent]. To this end was I born, and for this cause came I into the world, that I should bear witness unto the Truth." Pilate, it is true, could not follow Him in this train of thought, because he did not know what the truth was. To him, it was the most unreal thing imaginable.

He was thinking of the truth as something which the scholars of his day were vainly guessing after. What, then, could he think of One who rested His claims of royalty on being the living witness to the truth?

Let us not pass lightly over these words of the Christ. There have been good men, and wise men; there have been those whom we, in our enthusiasm, have called true men, — men who were faithful to a principle higher than themselves. But there has been but One who could or ever did say, "I am the Truth;" only One who could identify Himself with that infinite order and wisdom which guides all things. Think of it! He, in His Humanity, the perfect embodiment of Truth, — that which, to our little intelligences, seems so boundless, so unfathomable, so grand, so all-conquering. He, the Son of Man, the spent and weary One, the Truth, — the Word made flesh! What though Pilate spoke for an empire whose savage power would crush Him, unresisting, as a man would crush a flower! Did ever man "drest in a little brief authority," seem more insignifi-

cant, as, troubled and baffled by his gentle prisoner, he broke out angrily, " Speakest Thou not
unto me? Knowest Thou not that I have power
to crucify Thee, and have power to release Thee ? "
Do these bragging words deceive us ? Do we
not see that if Christ is the Truth, if He did in-
corporate into His Humanity everything of that
order and wisdom we pretend to reverence, that
then, however shamefully men abuse Him, however loudly they hoot at Him, however tightly
they nail Him, He, the silent, the suffering One,
has yet a majesty all His own, and is forever
" King of kings and Lord of lords " ?

And this, too, notwithstanding He stands there
clothed in our form and nature. Yet here is
where many stumble. They cannot but associate
weakness and sin with human nature. A Humanity which is perfect and divine, and therefore
omnipotent, is to them impossible. This is no
new perplexity. In the early days of the Christian
Church some were led to deny the reality of the
incarnation on this very ground.[1] To them, the

[1] See Note D.

assumption of Humanity was, in a certain way, degrading to the Divine Essence. But, as has been pointed out, the most spiritual of the apostles was the most strenuous in demanding faith in what we must call the materialism of Christ's Humanity. "That which we have heard, which we have seen with our eyes, which we have looked upon, and our hands have handled of the Word of Life, declare we unto you." John will have nothing less. "Every spirit that confesseth not that Jesus Christ is come in the flesh, is not of God; and this is that spirit of Antichrist, whereof ye have heard that it should come." Here, then, apparently, are two things to be reconciled:

Christ was human;

Christ was divine.

One fact is put just as strongly as the other. Weariness, temptation, suffering, — these, certainly, are emphasized; yet not more so than absolute sinlessness, perfection, and an infinitude of love, wisdom, and power such as do not belong to mortal man. Are the two facts irreconcilable? Not if we accept Christ's declaration that His Humanity became glorified, that is, made divine. "Now is the Son of Man glorified; and God is glorified in Him. If God be glorified in Him, God shall also glorify Him in Himself and shall straightway glorify Him." Thus "He glorified His Humanity by uniting it with the Divinity of which it was begotten." He did not take a Humanity merely to live in it for a short time, and at the end of that time cast it aside and be no more to man than He was before. The Humanity was assumed, that by means of the indwelling Divinity it (the Humanity) might be glorified with a divine glory and be made divine. For if the Humanity always remained frail and imperfect as at birth, the Jews had a measure of right in challenging His divine claims. If He, a finite though pure man, took upon Himself the divine prerogative of forgiving sin, was their indignation so culpable? If He was not really and absolutely divine, was it so strange that they were angered by His extraordinary claims, and resisted Him to the death?

"If I had not come," He said, "and spoken unto them, they had not had sin; but now they have no cloak for their sin." And He also said, "If I had not done among them the works which none other man did, they had not had sin; but now they have both seen and hated both Me and My Father," — that is, both the Humanity and the Divinity.

"I and my Father are one," He said to them one day. How did they answer Him? They took up stones to stone Him for blasphemy. But He stopped them and said: "Many good works have I shown you; for which of those works do ye stone Me?" And they answered angrily, "For a good work we stone Thee not; but for blasphemy; and [mark the words] because that Thou, being a man, makest Thyself God." "Because that Thou, being a man, makest Thyself God!" That was the issue. That is the issue now; and God pity us if we are still on the side of His enemies, who stood confronting Him with stones in their hands!

"Behold the Man!" He Himself exclaimed as

He, wounded and condemned, came forth to the
chief priests and officers. Our Gospels take away
much of the force of this memorable exclamation
by putting it into the mouth of Pilate. But
Pilate's name, being in italics, is an insertion of
the translators; and the passage should really
read: "Then came Jesus forth, wearing the
crown of thorns, and the purple robe; and saith
unto them, 'Behold the Man!'" The words are
Christ's. He presents Himself as the perfect,
the universal, the Divine Man. We do not forget
that He came fresh from the scourging, and that
His visage must have been marred indeed. We
do not forget that He came out wearing "the sad
finery" with which the soldiers had decked Him.
No doubt they were still laughing over their cruel
sport, and pointing their guilty fingers at the
thorn-crowned King. But He stood there calm
and gentle amid that storm of ridicule and hate;
stood there and made one exclamation to them, —
nay, to the universe of worlds, —"Ἴδε ὁ ἀνθρω-
πος! ("Behold the Man!") *The* man, — not
a man, — the one, perfect, God-Man! Bereft of

friends, scourged, ridiculed, condemned, but still the Man!

There was but one answer to this exclamation of the crowned Messiah. It was full of hate. " Crucify Him! " cried the chief priests and officers, — " Crucify Him! " Nothing shall save Him now, — not even the timid remonstrance of Pilate, " Shall I crucify your King? " It was because He would not be the king they secretly longed for, and because His kingdom was not of this world, that they took Him away and crucified Him.[1] Had He been a king to lead them forth against their enemies, as in the days of old, they would have drawn their swords for Him. Because His kingship was spiritual, they were well content to see Him pierced. And they only betrayed themselves when they came and complained to Pilate, " Write not, ' The King of the Jews; ' but that He said, ' I am King of the Jews.' "

It was indeed as the Lord said: they knew not what they were doing. They saw no majesty in the Prince of Peace. But the time came when

[1] See Note E.

the Lord, in a divinely spiritual body, ascended into heaven. And there His Humanity shines eternally. In the city of God, the Lamb is the Light thereof. When the scenery of the Isle of Patmos melted away before John in his banishment, and the landscapes of the spirit-world came floating before his inner senses, he looked, and lo! among the heavenly lights, walking amid the golden lamps, was "One like unto the Son of Man." No longer despised and rejected, the crucified One shone in His eternal majesty. "His head and His hairs were white like wool, as white as snow; and His eyes were as a flame of fire; and His feet like unto fine brass, as if they burned in a furnace. . . . And His countenance was as the sun shineth in his strength."

A vision sublime, almost awful in its glory, so that John fell in deadly fear at His feet. And yet the central light of those golden lamps was like unto the Son of Man. John feels that he is lying at his Master's feet; only the material coverings have been burned away, and the Humanity of his Saviour shines out in divine

12

majesty and glory. The Son of Man, no longer spent and weary, as when John followed Him amid the hills of Palestine, but "clothed with light inaccessible, girt with omnipotence and love!" Worshipped by the heavenly hosts, yet still revealing Himself as the Son of Man, — God in Humanity; God manifest in Jesus Christ.

"Thou art my King, —
My King henceforth alone;
And I, thy servant, Lord, am all Thine own.
Give me Thy strength; oh, let Thy dwelling be
In this poor heart that pants, my Lord, for Thee!"

THE SACRIFICE OF CHRIST.

" When my love for Christ grows weak,
When for stronger faith I seek,
Hill of Calvary, I go
To thy scenes of fear and woe:
Then to life I turn again,
Learning all the worth of pain,
Learning all the might that lies
In a full self-sacrifice."

Helps by the Way.

VIII.

The Sacrifice of Christ.

✠

*" I lay down My life, that I might take it again.
No man taketh it from Me, but I lay it down of
Myself. I have power to lay it down, and I have
power to take it again."*

✠

" HE saved others, Himself He cannot save ! "
Such was the cruel taunt of Christ's per-
secutors. The cross with its sacred burden had
been raised, and fallen into its socket; the male-
factors had entered upon their agony, and were
on either side of Him ; and when the chief priests
and the scribes and the elders saw Him, as they
believed, conquered, — saw Him really nailed to
the cross, all helpless against their indignities,
held there by the iron nails, powerless, friendless,

their prisoner, their victim, — they gave vent to
what was doubtless a shout of relief.

For always men try to bolster themselves in
their weakest part.   So, when the crisis came,
and they found they had nothing to fear; when
they found He did not baffle or escape them by
superhuman power; then this fear, which had
been lying on their consciences, betrayed itself
in that exultant cry, "He saved others, Himself
He cannot save!"

And the thieves on either side of Him, with
their nerves stretched in pain, and desperate in
their agony, — they, too, turned on Him; and one
of them reviled Him, and took up the taunt that
kept swelling up to that central cross, and said,
"If Thou be Christ, save Thyself and us."   And
the disciples stood apart, watching the sad scene
despairing; and the women were weeping; and
the people were mocking and wagging their
heads; and the despised and the rejected One
bore all in love and patience, and let the taunt
go unanswered, — let it go down the ages un-
reproved and uncontradicted, — for it carried a

truth, the truth which He came to establish, the truth of self-sacrifice. "He saved others, Himself He cannot save!"

Those who mocked, meant, of course, that He was helpless; that, like ·Samson for instance, He had proved weak at last, and that there was now no power on earth or in heaven which could come and snatch Him from His place. How false this was He had already shown : once to Peter, when He said at His arrest, "Thinkest thou I cannot now pray to My Father, and He shall presently give Me more than twelve legions of angels?" And once to Pilate, when He asserted His kingly strength with such gentle dignity : "My kingdom is not of this world; if My kingdom were of this world, then would My servants fight that I should not be delivered to the Jews; but now is My kingdom not from hence."

The meaning of the mob was false, but the words were true. He who had come to save others, nay, He who had saved others, must Himself perish; for their salvation was through

His self-sacrifice. "Greater love hath no man than this, that a man lay down his life for his friends." He, the very Truth itself, could not do less than fulfil His own words. "Whosoever shall seek to save his life shall lose it; and whosoever shall lose his life shall preserve it." "I lay down my life," He said, — and there are no words more impressive, — "I lay down my life that I may take it again. No man taketh it from Me, but I lay it down of Myself. I have power to lay it down, and I have power to take it again."

Now, we may often have wondered why Christ's death was a necessity. Why should He to whom we all look as in some sense divine, suffer a death so shameful as to be "reckoned among the transgressors"? Why should He be maligned, and scourged, and spit upon, and nailed to a cross, — He who spake as never man spake; He whom no one could convince of sin; who only did good?

Questions like these bring us face to face with one of the most solemn truths of the

Christian religion. The sacrifice of Christ is the touchstone of theology. Especially does it test our belief in two primal facts of our common faith: the Divinity of Christ, and the Unity of God. In a word, our conception of the sacrifice of Christ will determine both by name and by quality the form of our Christianity.

It is not a mere point of doctrine that we seek to raise. For ourselves and for our friends it is the living, rather than the theological, Christ that is needed. But how shall we follow Christ unless we know Him? and how shall we know Him unless we study Him, and try to understand His nature, and the purpose of His life and of His death? Christ as a name will not seriously affect us. Christ as a sentiment only, will not always hold us. Let us, indeed, seek the living Christ. Let us not think that we have Him, when it is only a theological image of Him we are embracing; but let us at least know Him when we find Him. Let us enter into the meaning and spirit of His redemption and of His sacrifice.

Now, we have this to encourage us, — that there are two facts which all Christians may hold in common; namely, that man, in his slavery to evil, needed to be redeemed, and that Christ accomplished that redemption.

Expanding these two facts, we can say that by sin man had separated himself from God, — separated himself by such a distance that he was in danger of losing his spiritual life and nature; and on the other hand, that Christ by His life and death brought man into restored relations with God. So far as we know, every Christian denomination would agree to these statements. "Further than those two essentials of the doctrine of atonement," declares a writer, " the acknowledgment of its necessity, and the belief in its virtual accomplishment in Christ, no systematic statement of the doctrine can be found in the early ages of the Christian Church."

Think of the days in which the Saviour came. Imagine the greater part of the civilized world to be under the most frightful despotism. Civil freedom is unknown. Each man lives in dread of the possible treachery of his neighbor. Society is diseased at the roots. Chastity and honor are openly ridiculed. Religion has either dwindled into the merest superstition, or hardened to a rigid formalism. And then if we could draw aside the veil, we would see the hosts of the infernal world crouching behind all these abuses and ready in an instant more to quite destroy humanity.

Who, now, can redeem this world? Who can make so much as an impression on it? Who can convince men of their sins? Who can shame them of their lusts? Who, in the midst of such spiritual blindness and unbelief, can restore men to a life of faith? Another Socrates? A soldier-hero, to raise the cry of "Reform!" amid the streets of Rome, and, if need be, enforce it at the point of the sword?

But the Saviour that did come! This simple, gentle Being, walking unattended to John's baptism! This plain, unknown Teacher from despised Nazareth! This "carpenter," as the people rated Him! This "man of sorrows"! This "Lamb of God"!

When Abraham climbed the sides of Mount Moriah, torch in hand, conducting his son to what he supposed would be his death, the lad, bearing the wood for his own pyre, asked in his child's simplicity, " My father, behold the fire and the wood, but where is the lamb for a burnt-offering ? " And the father of his people answered, " My son, God will provide Himself a lamb for a burnt-offering." And God did indeed provide Himself a lamb. For when He bowed the heavens and came to earth, He provided Himself a Humanity ; and this Humanity, which He sanctified and made divine, was the true " Lamb of God." In every respect the Humanity of our Lord answers to this figure. That it was sinless, loving, " meek and lowly in heart," we all believe.

And how did this " Lamb " take away the sin of the world ? The expression " take away " is translated " beareth " in the margin of our Gospels. " Behold the Lamb of God which beareth the sin of the world." Was it not by bearing, that sin could alone be taken away ? This does not mean that Christ, according to any conception of Him, abolished sin, — for is it not with us still? But He did bear it. In the language of prophecy, He did bear our griefs, and carry our sorrows, that by bearing and overcoming them in Himself, He, drawing personally nearer to us, might help us to bear and overcome.

How little the people about Him understood what He was doing. To many, " He had no form or comeliness that they should desire Him." And so they nailed Him to a cross, and mocked Him. And teachers have said that by this death God was reconciled to the world; when yet the apostle says that " God was in Christ, reconciling the world to Himself."

And then, too, what is the idea of sacrifice? Must we go back to the time when altars reeked with blood, and believe that the slaying of an animal or of a human being is pleasing to God, or accepted as a propitiation for sin? " Will the Lord be pleased with thousands of rams, or with ten thousands of rivers of oil? " Was Christ's sacrifice of this nature?

The Hebrew ordinances were, as the apostle describes them, "shadows of heavenly things." They all refer to Christ, — not, however, in the sense that they were to be literally reproduced in Him, but spiritually fulfilled. Take this very law of the sacrifice. What does sacrifice mean? Killing? Not at all. The slaying of the animal was only the symbol of the spiritual truth back of the sacrifice. And what is that? The word "sacrifice" means, to make holy. That which is set apart, and devoted to God; that which is made pure and holy to Him, is true sacrifice. "The sacrifices of God are a broken spirit; a broken and a contrite heart, O God, Thou wilt not despise." "I beseech you, brethren," cries the apostle, "by the mercies of God, that ye present your bodies a living sacrifice, holy, acceptable unto God, which is your reasonable service." This is not a plea for death, but for life, — a holy, consecrated life, wherein the body is day by day offered to God a true sacrifice.

To represent this spiritual consecration, the

Jews, who must needs have a literal, material basis for everything of religion, offered up certain animals upon their altars; for by this means they were literally set apart to God. And the Saviour was a sacrifice; for He declared that He sanctified Himself. He made His Humanity — that "Lamb" which bore the sins of the world — pure, holy, and divine. And in doing this He endured suffering, temptation, and even death. It was a daily sacrifice; the daily putting down of everything that was earth-born in subjection to the Divine within. So the Humanity became divine, — a living sacrifice. The death of Christ was only a part, or, rather, the solemn culmination of that work of sanctification which had been going on silently by day and by night for years. As such it was a necessity.

And in this idea of sacrifice is there not something that appeals to our deepest feelings and experiences? It is not always the man who marches bravely to physical death, who makes the greatest sacrifice. It is one thing for one to die with the eyes of the world upon him, and their cheers quickening him, and the struggle of kindred souls firing him to a courage which rushes openly upon death. It is another thing to struggle and die alone: to sacrifice time, pleasure, glory even, for ends which others look coldly on, or do not so much as understand; *to sacrifice self*, with all that that implies of self-abnegation, the patient endurance of sorrow and disappointment, the struggle and the victory over temptation, — in a word, the laying down little by little of the selfish, carnal life for the sake of the heavenly, the eternal life.

There have been souls who have lived and died for others; self-denying souls, who found their highest happiness in serving others; calm, trustful souls, who learned to bear the heaviest load for the Master's sake; true, heroic souls, who endured that highest martyrdom which any can undergo, — persecution for righteousness' sake. Many a home in our land contains sacrifices of this kind. And they are always sacred, though only God should see the sacrifice. And does the truth lose any of its force if we apply it to the

Saviour? He did infinitely what we can only do finitely. He, the Good Shepherd, did indeed lay down His life for the sheep.

But it may be said : Granting that sacrifice does mean to make sacred or holy, and that Christ, because He sanctified His Humanity by suffering, temptation, and death, was a true sacrifice, how did that avail in the restoration of man? The answer is, by uniting God and man through this Humanity as a medium, reconciling, or bringing them at-one-ment.

And this the Humanity of Christ is constantly doing. There is a high and holy life above us; there are ideals of greatness, purity, and devotion which seem always beyond us; there are the heavens, and the angels in those heavens, and the Father of that holy household, who keeps saying, " Be ye perfect, as your Father in heaven is perfect," — this on the one side of our nature, the side which has its windows towards God, and sees, as in a vision, the possibilities of a consecrated life; the peace, and glory, and ecstasy of those who become sanctified in the Lord, — and

13

on the other, the greed, the lust, the cruelties and
wrongs, the daily deceptions and snares, which
seem to cut off heaven by infinite distances, and
leave us in our own gross darkness.

It is not necessary to think of divine wrath as
standing over against this moral baseness of the
world. It is not necessary to think of Christ
as a separate person from God, trying by means
of prayers and the sight of His wounds to inter-
cept the divine judgments; trying to make the
Infinite One more merciful than He is, as though
He had not a heart to pity the sins and miseries
of a groaning world! Nowhere in the Scriptures
shall we find that such a mediation is necessary.
John in his old age looked with open vision upon
the bright scenery of heaven. He saw no monarch sitting on a throne, with lowering brow;
nothing to tell of divine wrath; but, as if to
prove to him the constancy and tenderness of the
divine love, though wounded by men's denials
and sins, he saw in the very midst of the throne,
— what? The stern Deity of our theologies?
No! He saw in the midst of that throne " A

Lamb as it had been slain;" as if, says one, "there was a Calvary not in Palestine alone, but away in the heart of God, where we crucify Him by our disobedience every day."

What we need, then, is not an intercessor, in the sense that God needs interceding, and as if, unless some one step in between us and the divine Judge, our cause is lost. What we do need, and what we have, is a medium, a channel between the infinite perfections of God and the vileness of man, such as will transmit the life of the former into the weakness and sicknesses of the latter; that God and man may not dwell apart, but be brought at one : man lifted up by repentance, to abide in the wisdom and love of the Lord; the Lord, living in the cleansed heart of the man. "And I [the Lord said], if I be lifted up, will draw all men unto Me." That was the true atonement, — the Lord glorifying His Humanity with the very divine love or fatherhood of His nature, and then raising men up into conjunction with Himself.

To this end He took upon Himself a nature like our own, — a nature which gave Him every appearance of being simply a man among men, but which was in direct communication with the Divine within. On the side of Humanity, it could touch men at their lowest; on the side of Divinity, it could be one with the infinite Jehovah.

Here, then, is no confusion of persons, but one infinite person clothed with our humanity, and making that Humanity a perfect medium for transmitting to men — poor, sinful, struggling men — such forms of the divine love and wisdom as they can receive. "Come unto Me!" the Saviour cried. We go to Him in His Divine Humanity, and lo! we find that everything of comfort or strength the weary soul can ask, comes from Him; comes, if we may so say, from some of His infinite experiences; comes from that perfect glorified Humanity in tides of sympathetic love and power. One such experience, and we shall be able to bear and answer

His question: "Believest thou not that I am in my Father, and my Father in Me?"

And how beautiful it is to look back to those hallowed years when our Saviour trod the earth, and know that back of that outward ministry, which, it would seem, must at times touch the hardest of us, this invisible work of sanctification was going on, — going on and never ceasing, — and a perfect medium, the Divine Humanity, was being prepared and provided for the comfort, ay, for the salvation of millions upon millions of troubled, tempted souls!

He had no place, the Gospels say, where to lay His head. With a love for the salvation of the whole world, He found but few to understand Him. Yet daily, hourly, He was living for them and laying down the life of His Humanity, that by sanctification He might be the world's perfect sacrifice. Persecution and crucifixion came; and He who had borne our griefs and carried our sorrows was jeered at; and the multitude hailed His approaching death with one exultant cry:

"He saved others, Himself He cannot save!"
The sacrifice was complete.

> "Jesu, meek and lowly,
> Saviour, pure and holy,
> On Thy love relying,
> Hear me humbly crying.

> "Prince of life and power,
> My salvation's tower,
> On the cross I view Thee,
> Calling sinners to Thee.

> "There behold me gazing
> At the sight amazing;
> Bending low before Thee,
> Helpless I adore Thee.

> "Fount of love unceasing,
> Whence is every blessing,
> All my aching sadness,
> Turn Thou into gladness.

> "Lord, in mercy guide me,
> Be Thou e'er beside me:
> In Thy ways direct me,
> 'Neath Thy wings protect me."

THE ETERNAL PRESENCE OF CHRIST.

What though I take to me the wide
  Wings of the morning and forth fly,
  Faster He goes, whose care on high
Shepherds the stars and doth them guide.

What though the tents foregone, I roam
  Till day wax dim lamenting me ;
  He wills that I shall sleep to see
The great gold stairs to His sweet home.

What though the press I pass before,
  And climb the branch, He lifts His face ;
  I am not secret from His grace
Lost in the leafy sycamore.

What though denied with murmuring deep
  I shame my Lord, — it shall not be ;
  For He will turn and look on me,
Then must I think thereon and weep.

The nether depth, the heights above,
  Nor alleys pleach'd of Paradise,
  Nor Herod's judgment-halls suffice :
Man shall not hide himself from love.

Holy Songs, Carols, and Sacred Ballads.

The Eternal Presence of Christ.

✠

"And lo! I am with you alway."

✠

FORTY days had elapsed since the great Day of Resurrection. While the story was being circulated that the disciples had come by night and stolen away their Master as He slept in the tomb, He in His resurrection body was coming and going among His believers, and raising their thoughts and affections to a distinctly higher plane than they had yet attained.

But at the end of the forty days, being once more with the apostles, He lifted up His hands and blessed them; and as He blessed them He was parted from them, and, in the simple language of the Gospels, was carried up into heaven.

And the apostles, we read, "worshipped Him, and returned to Jerusalem with great joy." Once His outward withdrawal had smitten them with a feeling of utter loneliness. But now the sorrow and fear had been overcome. They could better understand how the separation would only be in appearance, and that really and essentially He would remain within the sphere of their life, and be ever with them to support them in all their coming struggles. "I will see you again," He had promised them, "and your hearts shall rejoice, and your joy no man taketh from you." "I go away and come again unto you." "I will not leave you comfortless; I will come to you." With such promises in their hearts they could not think that He was leaving them.

And so when they saw Him enter the cloud, it was not dismay, nor even sorrow, that affected them, but joy. The conflicts were over. The world had been set free. The Son of Man had accomplished the work He came to do. Past were the pains, the toil, the weariness, which the flesh had endured; past, too, the temptation struggles in which the humanity had long engaged. Man had seen Him, heard Him, dwelt with Him. All that could be done by the contact of His Humanity with man's life had been accomplished. Yet the world still needed Him; and it needed Him most in that hidden power to uplift and save which comes in fulness from His Divine Humanity. And this is what He meant when He said to the disciples, " I tell you the truth: It is expedient for you that I go away: for if I go not away, the Comforter will not come unto you; but if I depart, I will send Him unto you." They were holding Him in their merely natural thoughts; He was preparing them to receive Him into their spiritual thoughts. He would ascend, but not separate Himself from them. Therefore He said to them, " Lo, I am with you alway."

Without that promise, they could not have fulfilled their mission as they did. For theirs was no easy task : to preach the Crucified as the very hope and strength of the soul, and to say to the hard and cruel masses that He whom they had scorned and put to death had ascended into heaven with power and great glory. These men, we must remember, were of a humble class. Most of them had, so to speak, just stepped out of their fishing-boats. The Lord Himself said they were "slow of heart." Apparently they were men of hard sense; they were severely literal; and it was no easy matter for them to understand Him or His teachings. Yet these unlettered men were to stand up before the sceptics, the cynics, the scholars of the day, and espouse a cause which not even the silvery eloquence of a Demosthenes could have made to prevail, without the Spirit of truth and the indwelling presence of the Lord.

Moreover, they must have known that their apostleship involved them in danger, persecution, and death. "They shall put you out of their synagogues," the Saviour said; "yea, the time cometh, that whosoever killeth you, will think that he doeth God service." "When thou shalt be old," He said to Simon Peter, "thou shalt stretch forth thine hands, and another shall gird thee, and carry thee whither thou wouldest not.

This spake He, signifying by what death He
should glorify God." He was signing the man
with the cross. It was to be a thrilling experience, this preaching of Jesus of Nazareth; and
nothing save a belief in His eternal presence
could have made the first Christian apostleship
that devoted service which compels our admiration. But if the disciples spoke and worked
from minds made sensitive by the breathings of
the Holy Ghost; if they lived in the faith that
the Lord was with them according to His promise,
"I will not leave you comfortless, I will come
to you," — then they had sources of power and
courage sufficient for all their needs.

When, on the day of Pentecost, Simon Peter
arose and preached the resurrection and saving
power of the Crucified with such unction that
three thousand souls were enrolled by baptism,
he spoke with lips which had been touched by
coals of fire from the altar of God. When he
arose, many were jeering and accusing the apostles
of drunkenness. But as the sermon went on
the jeers grew fainter; and soon the men were

crying out, "What shall we do?" And Peter said, "Repent, and be baptized, every one of you, in the name of Jesus Christ for the remission of sins, and ye shall receive the gift of the Holy Ghost." Surely, the Holy Spirit which filled the multitude on that day, and which has filled all true disciples ever since, was the spirit of the Lord Himself, then given in fulness, because His glorification was complete.

The work went on. But the priests and Sadducees, becoming maddened by this revival of the religion of Jesus, caused Peter and John to be cast into prison. The day following, they were brought before the Jewish rulers. There sat Annas the high priest, and Caiaphas, before whom another Prisoner had once stood bound, charged with blasphemy. "By what power, or by what name have ye done this?" they demanded. The time was when one of those prisoners had denied His Master with a curse, and fled from the high priest's palace in shame and dismay. But now he faced these hard judges without fear, being filled, says the narrative, with

the Holy Ghost, and in a few stirring sentences
drove their sin home. And they, "when they
saw the boldness of Peter and John, and perceived
that they were unlearned and ignorant men, marvelled." "Unlearned and ignorant" save in
that knowledge which had been hid from the
wise and prudent; and weak, but for the divine
strength which supported their honest hearts.

These incidents will suffice. They tell of the
presence of the Redeemer in the hearts of His
apostles, and the fulfilment of His promise, "Lo,
I am with you alway." Sore beset with difficulties, enduring privation and danger, they carried
on their mission in this supreme trust, that by
night or by day, in storm or in calm, the spirit
of their Lord was flowing out to them in streams
of strength and consolation. Nor was this new
influx of power confined to a few, but soon became "one of the divine signatures of Christianity generally, found all through the second
century, and always in connection with and
within the circle of Christian ideas and Christian
communions."

But we cannot stop with the second, nor even the third, century. This new spirit of life is for the ages. The presence of Christ is an eternal presence. It was not that He might withdraw Himself from Humanity, which struggles on from age to age, and, shining in His infinite perfections with a light sevenfold greater than the sun, merely dazzle us with His splendor, that He ascended into heaven. He has not come to men in His loving, human way, lived with them, suffered with them, taught them to look to Him as Friend, Comforter, Saviour, only that He might confound them at last with His glory. We surely have not read the story of His life aright, if we have not seen that He was sharing our human experiences in order that He might be an ever-present Saviour, — one who could say to the nineteenth as well as the first century, "Lo, I am with you alway."

And this, after all, is what we feel the need of most, — the divine life commingling with our human life; making us strong in its strength; guiding, rescuing, forgiving; winning its way to our hearts and consciences, and saving us from ourselves.

Now, there has always been among men this hope in the divine presence. "Whither shall I go from Thy Spirit," exclaims the Psalmist, "or whither shall I flee from Thy presence? If I ascend up into heaven, behold Thou art there; if I make my bed in hell, behold Thou art there." "My presence shall go with thee," the Lord said to Moses, "and I will give thee rest." To which Moses replied, "If Thy presence go not with me, carry us not up hence."

Centuries went by; and then there appeared a Being who had grown up in the silence of those mysterious years in Nazareth, even as the temple — type, as He declared, of His own body — grew silently, "with noiseless slide of stone to stone." A few came to Him; and they found in His presence a fulness of joy such as they had never felt before. It surely is one of the beautiful studies of the Gospels to see how men like His apostles became, as it were, lost in Him. He called, and they came. They left their boats

14

and their nets, and followed Him. They did not understand Him at the first. His words were often a sore puzzle to them; His acts constantly surprised them. But as the end draws near, we can feel how those men have been getting farther and farther into that mystic circle. They have learned to look to Him for wisdom and love. More and more He becomes a necessity to them; "Lord, to whom shall we go?" cried Peter; "Thou hast the words of eternal life." The man has found his refuge. How then could he go out from under the shadow of those wings!

And then the crash came. The disciples were scattered. The mock trial was soon over with; and the men who had loved Him, saw Him with His arms stretched upon a cross. Then the last spark of hope or courage seemed to go out. What was there left? Ah! there is a wonderful touch of pathos in that abrupt exclamation of Peter, after the crucifixion and burial: "I go a fishing." It is as if the man felt that the day-dreams were over, and that this new, strange life, which had for three years enfolded him, had ended in defeat, and there was nothing left for him now but the sea, and the boats, and the nets. And Peter's companions said, "We also go with thee." [1]

But the end was not yet. The disciples were rallied. Their Master moved among them once again; gave them a higher courage; turned their doubts into unwavering faith; and, as we have seen, sent them into the world with the assurance of His eternal presence. And millions of souls since then have lived in the faith that the Lord Jesus, although ascended into heaven, is not cut off from them, but is an ever-present Comforter and Saviour.

Take that thought away, and we take away the inspiration to be Christ-like. For to be like Him, yet be without Him; merely to model after Him, without the support of His actual presence, and without the strength to bear and endure flowing down from Him, — this were a hopeless task. "Without Me ye can do nothing."

[1] See Note F.

God, for the sake of our moral freedom, permits us to act as of ourselves. We may confirm this appearance to the point of believing that our power is self-derived. Thus Pilate, proud in his supposed strength, turned haughtily upon Jesus, and said, " Knowest Thou not that I have power to crucify Thee, and have power to release Thee ? " And how did the Lord answer him ? "Thou couldst have no power at all against Me, except it were given thee from above." The power even for evil, the power to abuse God's life, is granted from above, and granted in order that that which the evil prize equally with the good — the sense of freedom — may not be taken away.

In this fact we find an answer to one of those hard questions with which we sometimes vex ourselves. Why do we not continually have a distinct and unmistakable sense of the divine presence ? If the Lord is with us always, why do we not always feel it ? The answer is a simple one: because if such were the case, good would be done, not from choice, nor through motives of self-denial, but because, forsooth, we felt God

was shadowing us, and we durst not do otherwise! The Lord, therefore, permits His life to
appear to us as our life. Like the man in the
parable, He supplies us with gifts, and then
retires from view, in order that we may use these
gifts in freedom to our eternal advantage. But
the truth of it all is stated in that simple declaration of the Gospel: " A man can receive nothing
except it be given him from heaven." We cannot move a dust atom without the power of life
which comes from God. " In God we live, and
move, and have our being."

> "He is more present to all things He made,
> Than anything unto itself can be."

In reality, therefore, the appearance granted
to man of his separateness from God is the
greater miracle. And it is the mark of the
highest love. For God lives in the love of
blessing man with His perfect life, yet never
suffers that love to deprive man of the liberty to
receive or reject Him. He knocks, He calls,
but does not compel our hospitality. " Wilt
Thou that we command fire to come down from

heaven and consume them, even as Elias did?"
Such was the exclamation of James and John
when the Samaritans refused to receive Him into
their dwellings.   But He turned to the "sons
of thunder" and rebuked them, saying, "Ye
know not what manner of spirit ye are of."   And
they went to another village.

And yet there is no fact which is harder for
the merely natural man to understand than the
divine presence.   In the grossness of his concep-
tions he places God away off somewhere in space;
and then his problem is, how God can extend
Himself so as to be present bodily in all places
of the universe.

But the Lord's presence is a presence in the
soul.   It is the presence of His love and wisdom
in our affections and thoughts.   It is His spiritual indwelling, and not the contact of His divine
body with our material bodies.   God's life is
love, — pure, boundless, unceasing love.   It is not
a blind love; for it is united with wisdom, even
as the sun's heat clothes itself with light.   And
these two life-giving qualities go forth from Him

in His divine Humanity in infinite measures. They radiate as universally into our vast mind-realm as the heat and light of the material sun pour themselves forth into all things of the physical universe. And the question never can be, How can God be here, and there, and elsewhere? but, Where can I be that God's love and wisdom are not?

Our simile fails us in this: that the sun is material and impersonal, and hence the heat and light which issue from it are, in a sense, dead. But the love and wisdom of God are not dead, and they flow from a source supremely personal. If any tell us that infinite love and wisdom are everywhere about the souls of men, but that we know nothing of their source, and so just call these divine forces " God," the fact of the divine presence falls cold and dead upon our souls. Faith and love must have a personal object; and that object to a Christian should be Jehovah-Jesus, the Lord in His divine and glorified Humanity. And when we say that the divine omnipresence is through the infinite radiations of love and wisdom, it is in the belief that that love and wisdom are from the Lord God our Saviour. They are His life, the essences of His nature. For He said, "Lo, I am with you alway." That was the truth to the men who heard Him. That should be the truth to us, who have not seen and yet should believe. It is not so much sheer life, no one knows whence; it is the life of an infinite Lord, communicating itself through the love and wisdom which go forth from Him as real, life-giving essences, and which come to us out of His full knowledge of our special cares, and trials, and short-comings.

For while it is true that every life, pure or vile, is enfolded in the universal life of God, it would not be true to say that there is no ministration to personal needs; or that the divine presence can be no more to the man who is trying to open his inmost heart to Him, than to one whose heart seems riveted against Him. The difference is a vast one, and the sensations of the two men are vastly different. The Lord indicated the difference when He said, "If any man will hear My voice and open the door, I will come in to him, and sup with him, and he with Me." In any case, the Lord as to His divine life is there. Whether the man hears or not, whether he draws out the bolts or not, the Light of the world is there; but if a man is insensible to the yearnings and pleadings of that life, he derives no sense of pleasure from its presence.

This is a matter which belongs to the experience of every individual. If we fail in our duty; if we go contrary to the dictates of our conscience, and sin; why, then, surely, there is no thought or desire for the presence of the Lord. But let a man resist some evil thought or feeling as sinful before Him; let him do the duty which lies before him, even if laborious or repugnant, for His sake, and we appeal to the richest experiences of Christian hearts whether there does not come a sense of protection against the evil, and of joy in the good, such as cannot be of earth, but reveals the presence of the Lord. Enlarge such an experience so as to include all our experiences, and we should have this: a human life trying to open itself to the divine life, enduring such labor, conflict, trials, as came to it, with a belief in the reality and supremacy of the divine life; and as the result of this living faith, gaining, be it never so slowly, a certain strength and hero- ism of soul which makes a man calm though the storms are beating on him, and brings to him again and again the very peace of God.

This is not easy. God knows how the lusts of the flesh, and the chink of gold, and the calls of worldly ambitions entice us. And we show Him the door, and turn the lock, and push in the bolts; and then it is only self-gratification that we care or struggle for. Yet God could say, — ah! with such reproach, — "I am with you alway." As surely as we live, there come knockings at the door, — something appealing at our hearts which is not of man. It is the pres- ence of the Lord, who created from love, who sustains from love, and who saves from love.

Now, the Lord has pointed out certain means which the Christian may employ in securing the divine presence in its fulness.

"Where two or three are gathered together in

My name, there am I in the midst of them."
He was speaking of the united prayers of those
who believe in Him, and pledging them His
presence. And His words have proved an inspiration to Christian worshippers, who, whether
in the silence of their closets, or in the family
circle, or in consecrated buildings, have knelt
and prayed, even as His Humanity so often knelt
and prayed, and brought itself into conscious
union with the indwelling Fatherhood.

Then, at the close of His ministry, He insti-
tuted the Holy Supper as the most sacred means
of coming into union with Him. "This do in
remembrance of Me," He said to the men gathered about Him. "In remembrance of Me."
And many a company since that night have come
together, and partaken of elements like unto those
which He distributed as the symbols of His divine body and blood. And wherever they have
come together in faith to the Lord and charity
to the neighbor, there the Lord their Redeemer
has been present with them both as to His
Divinity and as to His glorified Humanity.

And one more command He gave: "Search
the Scriptures; for in them ye think ye have
eternal life, and they are they which testify of
Me." All through the Gospels it is pointed out
how He fulfilled the sacred Scriptures. The
brazen serpent, raised upon a pole in the wilderness, proved to be a sign of the lifting up of the
Son of Man. The entombment of Jonah in the
whale's belly, is the prefigurement of the Son
of Man being "three days and three nights in
the heart of the earth." The piercing of His
hands and feet, the parting of His garments,
the lots cast for His seamless vesture, the gall
and the vinegar thrust to His dying lips, the
mockings and revilings around the cross, — all
had been foretold in the Psalms of David. The
testimony of Jesus is indeed the spirit of prophecy.
The Christian Bible is not simply the book of
sublime ideas and philosophies; it is the Book
of Jesus Christ. In its histories are inscribed
the spiritual experiences of His life among men.
"These are the words which I spake unto you,"
He said after His resurrection, "while I was yet

with you; that all things must be fulfilled which
were written in the law of Moses, and in the
Prophets, and in the Psalms, concerning Me."
" And beginning at Moses and all the Prophets,
He expounded to them in all the Scriptures the
things concerning Himself."

In the light of these statements, what a thrilling, divinely-human book the Bible becomes!
What earnest disciple, whether in this or in the
early centuries, has not longed to know more of
the inner life of Jesus Christ than the Gospels,
in their letter, disclose? Who, we may ask
reverently, has not wished to know more of the
heart of Christ, — the yearnings that were beating
there; the thoughts that were encircling the tot-
tering lives of men; the pains, the fierce assaults
of evil, that made Him indeed "a man of sorrows"! And now if it be really true that the
secrets of this most sacred and pathetic of all
histories are treasured up in the Christian's
Bible, is it not in that Bible that we may hope
to meet Him? " The words that I speak unto
you, they are spirit and they are life." Some-

thing of heaven and of God will ever flow out
to men from these sacred pages ; something which
the best text-books of history, or science, or of
ethics never have given, nor ever can give them ;
something which lies behind its most obscure
symbols, and is as much beyond the reach of the
lance of the critic as the soul is beyond the
scalpel of the anatomist.   In dark trial-hours
many a devout soul has found the Bible the
medium of divine life and consolation.   But the
supreme and perfect cause of its holy power was
revealed in the declarations and example of the
Christ, who held up the Scriptures for reverence,
and who told the world that whether in the form
of history, or psalmody, or prophecy, they contained the story of His life.   They are the vehi-
cle of the divine life.   "Did not our heart burn
within us while He talked with us by the way,
and while He opened to us the Scriptures?"
And in this exchange of confidence between the
two men who walked to Emmaus on the evening
of the resurrection is revealed the secret of the
power of that Word which once in the history

of the world "was made flesh and dwelt among us, full of grace and truth."

> "And so the Word had breath, and wrought
> With human hands the creed of creeds,
> In loveliness of perfect deeds,
> More strong than all poetic thought."

And we keep looking back to those deeds; we keep looking to that figure, simply clad, as it moves among the hills and valleys of Palestine, the Friend of publicans and sinners, — a figure of beauty and sweet majesty going and coming among men, full of pity for their ignorances, full of sorrow for their sins. A little company are gathered round Him, — simple, devoted men and women. They follow Him from place to place; they watch His miracles; they listen to His teachings. Sometimes they grow perplexed, and look questioningly into His face; sometimes the peace of His divine life brings them heavenly content. Then He is withdrawn from outward view. But "in the dense and general darkness little communions called churches arise, dotting the regions of night like spangles of gold and silver."

The years roll on, and still that name is on men's lips; the story of that life is told over and over. At the end of more than eighteen centuries we are studying the footprints of the Saviour. Through daily tasks and trials we are trying to walk in those footprints; for they are the marks of God's Humanity. And that Humanity, shining in divine glory, is with us now and forever. It answers all our needs. It meets us in joy and sorrow, in peace and temptation, in life and in death. In its power against evil, in its holy strengthening spirit, it is fulfilling the promise from age to age, " Lo, I am with you alway."

> "No fable old, nor mythic lore,
>   Nor dream of bards and seers,
> No dead fact stranded on the shore
>   Of the oblivious years;
>
> " But warm, sweet, tender, even yet
>   A present help is He;
> And faith has still its Olivet,
>   And love its Galilee.
>
> "The healing of His seamless dress
>   Is by our bed of pain;
> We touch Him in life's throng and press
>   And we are whole again.

"Through Him the first fond prayers are said
  Our lips of childhood frame ;
The last low whispers of our dead
  Are burdened with His name.

.   .   .   .

" So, to our mortal eyes subdued
  Flesh-veiled, but not concealed,
We know in Thee the Fatherhood
  And heart of God revealed."

15

NOTES.

NOTES.

Note A. — Page 34.

Stated by the Rev. C. Ginsburg in "The Bible Educator." So also the Talmud: "After the completion of the twelfth year a boy is to be considered a youth, and is to keep the fast on the Day of Atonement. Till he is thirteen his religious duties are to be performed for him by his father; but on his thirteenth birthday the parent is no longer answerable for his son's sins." Quoted in Geikie's "Life and Words of Christ."

Note B. — Page 34.

Suggested by Eugene Stock in "Lessons on the Life of our Lord," Ginsburg, and others.

Note C. — Page 134.

The author of "Ecce Homo" states the matter thus: "As with Socrates argument is everything and personal authority nothing, so with Christ personal authority is all in all and argument altogether unemployed. As Socrates is never tired of depreciating himself and dissembling his own superiority to those with whom he converses, so Christ perpetually and persistently exalts himself. As Socrates firmly denies what all admit, and explains away what the oracle had announced, namely, his own superior wisdom, so Christ steadfastly asserts what many were not

prepared to admit, namely, his own absolute superiority
to all men and his natural title to universal royalty."

NOTE D. — Page 171.

"Now, He suffered all these things for us: and He
suffered them really, and not in appearance only, even
as also He truly rose again. But not, as some of the
unbelievers, who are ashamed of the formation of man,
and the cross, and death itself, affirm, that in appearance
only, and not in truth, He took a body of the Virgin, and
suffered only in appearance, forgetting, as they do, Him
who said, 'The Word was made flesh;' and again,
'Destroy this temple, and in three days I will raise
it up.'" — Ignatius (about 107 A. D.), "Epistle to the
Smyrnæans."

"But if, not having been made flesh, He did appear as
if flesh, His work was not a true one. But what He did
appear, that He also was: God recapitulated in Himself
the ancient formation of man, that He might kill sin,
deprive death of its power, and vivify man; and therefore
His words are true." Irenæus (A. D. 120–202), "Against
Heresies," Book iii.

"But how will all this be true in Him, if He was not
Himself true, — if He really had not in Himself that which
might be crucified, might die, might be buried, and might
rise again? *I mean* this flesh suffused with blood, built
up with bones, interwoven with nerves, entwined with
veins, *a flesh* which knew how to be born and how to die,
human without doubt, as born of a human being. . . . The
powers of the Spirit proved Him to be God, His sufferings attested the flesh of man. If His powers were not

without the Spirit, in like manner were not His sufferings without the flesh. If this flesh with its sufferings was fictitious, for the same reason was the Spirit false, with all its powers. Wherefore halve Christ with a lie? He was wholly the truth." — Tertullian (A. D. 145–220), "On the Flesh of Christ."

Note E. — Page 176.

"[Christ] understood the work of the Messiah in one sense, [the Jews] in another, but what was the point of irreconcilable difference? They laid information against him before the Roman government as a dangerous character; their real complaint against him was precisely this, that he was *not* dangerous. Pilate executed him on the ground that his kingdom was of this world; the Jews procured his execution precisely because he was not. In other words, they could not forgive him for claiming royalty and at the same time rejecting the use of physical force." — Ecce Homo, ch. iii.

Note F. — Page 211.

See a sermon by the Rev. Robert Collyer on "Why Simon Peter went A-fishing," published in *The Every Other Saturday*, July 19, 1884.

Note G.

The doctrine of the Son of Man contained in this book is that which is elaborated in the theological writings of Swedenborg. To him the entire Scriptures were the revelation of one great central truth, — the supreme divinity of the Lord Jesus Christ.

Messrs. ROBERTS BROTHERS'

LIST OF

RELIGIOUS PUBLICATIONS.

ALGER (W. R.)　A Critical History of the Doctrine
of a Future Life.　With Bibliography.　8vo. . . . . .　3.50
Prayers offered in the Massachusetts House of Rep-
resentatives during the Session of 1868.　16mo. . .　1.50

ALLEN (JOSEPH HENRY).　Hebrew Men and
Times.　From the Patriarchs to the Messiah.　A new,
revised Edition.　16mo. . . . .　1.50
Fragments of Christian History.　16mo. . . . . . .　1.25
Christian History in its Three Great Periods: First
Period, Early Christianity; Second Period, the Middle Age;
Third Period, Modern Phases.　3 vols.　16mo. . . . .　3.75
Our Liberal Movement in Theology, chiefly as shown in
Recollections of the History of Unitarianism in New Eng-
land.　16mo. . . . .　1.25

ARNOLD (EDWIN).　The Light of Asia; or, the
Great Renunciation: being the Life and Teaching of
Gautama, Prince of India and Founder of Buddhism.
16mo. . . . . ' . . .　1.00

BARTOL (C. A.)　Radical Problems.　16mo. . . . .　2.00
The Rising Faith.　16mo.. . . . .　2.00
Principles and Portraits.　(Dr. Bartol's "Portraits" include Shakespeare, Channing, Bushnell, Weiss, Garrison
and Wm. M. Hunt.)　16mo. . . . .　2.00

BLESSED LIFE (THE).　Favorite Hymns, selected by
the Editor of "Quiet Hours."　Square 18mo. . . . .　1.00

CHADWICK (J. W.)　The Faith of Reason.　A Series
of Discourses on the Leading Topics of Religion.　16mo.　1.00
The Man Jesus.　16mo. . . . .　1.00

CHANNING (WILLIAM ELLERY, D. D.)　The
Perfect Life.　In Twelve Discources.　Edited from his
Manuscripts by his nephew, William Henry Channing.
12mo. . . . .　1.50

CHILD (LYDIA MARIA).　Aspirations of the World.
A Chain of Opals.　16mo. . . . .　1.25

CHRIST AND MODERN THOUGHT.　Being the
New Volume of "Boston Monday Lectures," with a pre-
liminary Lecture by Joseph Cook.　16mo.. . . . . .　1.50

COLLIER (R. LAIRD).　Meditations on the Essence
of Christianity.　12mo. . . . .　1.25

DIVINITY OF CHRIST. An Examination of Canon Liddon's Bampton Lectures on the Divinity of our Lord and Saviour Jesus Christ. By a Clergyman of the Church of England. 12mo. 1.75

EVERETT (WILLIAM). School Sermons preached to the Boys of Adams Academy, Quincy, Mass. 1 vol. 16mo. 1.00

FARIS (WILLIAM W.). The Children of Light. (Second Fletcher Prize Essay). 16mo. 1.50

FAUNCE (D. W.) The Christian in the World. (First Fletcher Prize Essay). 1.50

FREEDOM AND FELLOWSHIP IN RELIGION. With an Introduction by Rev. O. B. Frothingham. 16mo. 1.50

GRIFFIN (R. ANDREW). From Traditional to Rational Faith ; or, The Way I Came from Baptist to Liberal Christianity. 1.00

HALE (EDWARD E.). The Life in Common. Sermons. 16mo. 1.25
The Kingdom of God. Sermons. 16mo. 1.25
June to May. Sermons. 16mo. . . . . - . 1.25

HALE (LUCRETIA P.). The Lord's Supper, and its Observance. 16mo. 1.00

HEAVEN SERIES (THE). Heaven our Home. Life in Heaven. Meet for Heaven. 3 vols. 16mo. Each 1.00

HEDGE (F. H.). The Primeval World of Hebrew Tradition. 16mo. 1.50
Reason in Religion. 16mo. 1.50
Ways of the Spirit, and other Essays. 16mo. . . . 1.50

HOLY SONGS, CAROLS AND SACRED BALLADS. An original work by an eminent English Poet. Square 16mo. 1.00

INGRAHAM (J. H.) The Prince of the House of David ; or, Three Years in the Holy City. 12mo. . . . 2.00
The Pillar of Fire ; or, Israel in Bondage. 12mo. . . . 2.00
The Throne of David,—from the Consecration of the Shepherd of Bethlehem to the Rebellion of Prince Absalom. 12mo. 2.00

JACOX (FRANCIS). Cues from all Quarters ; or, Literary Musings of a Clerical Recluse. 16mo. 1.50
Bible Music : Being Variations in many Keys on Musical Themes from Scripture. 12mo. 1.75

KNAPPERT (J.). The Religion of Israel: A Manual. Translated from the Dutch by Richard A. Armstrong. 16mo. 1.00

MARTINEAU (JAMES). Hours of Thought on Sacred things. First Series. 16mo. 1.50
Second Series. 12mo. 2.00

ONESIMUS. Memoirs of a Disciple of St. Paul. By the author of "Philochristus." 16mo. 1.50

OORT (DR. H.) and HOOYKAAS (DR. I.). The Bible for Learners. Translated from the Dutch by Rev. P. H. Wicksteed of London. With a comprehensive Index, made especially for this Edition, and Maps.
The Old Testament. 2 vols. 12mo. 4.00
The New Testament. 1 vol. 12mo. 2.00

PARKER (JOSEPH). Ecce Deus: Essays on the Life and Doctrine of Jesus Christ. With Controversial Notes on "Ecce Homo." 16mo.. . . . .   1.50
Ad Clerum: Advices to a Young Preacher. 16mo. . . .   1.50

PARKER (THEODORE), Prayers. A new edition with Preface by Louisa M. Alcott, and a Memoir by F. B. Sanborn. 16mo. 1.00
Lessons from the World of Matter and the World of Man. Selected from notes of unpublished sermons, by Rufus Leighton. (*A quite limited edition*). 430 pages. Steel Portrait. 12mo. 1.50

PARSONS (THEOPHILUS). The Infinite and the Finite. 16mo. 1.00
Outlines of the Religion and Philosophy of Swedenborg. 16mo. 1.25

PAUL OF TARSUS. An Inquiry into the Times and the Gospel of the Apostle of the Gentiles. By a Graduate. 16mo. 1.50

PEABODY (A. P.). Christian Belief and Life. 16mo.   1.50

PHILOCHRISTUS. Memoirs of a Disciple of the Lord. 16mo. 1.50

POWERS (N. H.). Through the Year. 16mo. . . .   1.50

PUTNAM (A. P.). Singers and Songs of the Liberal Faith. 8vo. 3.00

QUIET HOURS. A Collection of Poems. Square 18mo. First and Second Series each. 1.00
"   "   "   " two volumes in one. 16mo. . .   1.50

ROSSETTI (CHRISTINA G.). Annus Domini: A
Prayer for Each Day of the Year. Square 18mo. . . . 1.50

SCHEFER (LEOPOLD). The Layman's Breviary.
Square 16mo. $2.25. A cheaper edition, ... 1.50
The World-Priest. Square 16mo. . . . . , 2.25

SEELEY (J. R.). Ecce Homo. A Survey of the Life
and Work of Jesus Christ. 16mo. $1.50. A cheaper
edition. 1.00
Roman Imperialism, and other Lectures and Essays.
16mo. 1.50

SUNSHINE IN THE SOUL. Poems, selected by the
Editor of "Quiet Hours." 18mo. 50

SUPERNATURAL RELIGION. An Inquiry into the
Reality of Divine Revelation. To which is added the
Author's Preface to the sixth edition. 3 vols. 8vo. . . 12.50

SURSUM CORDA. Hymns for the Sick and Suffering,
compiled by the Editor of "Quiet Hours," "Sunshine in
the Soul," etc. 16mo. 1.25

TAYLER (JOHN JAMES). Last Series of Christian
Aspects of Faith and Duty. Square 12mo. 2.00

WALKER (JAMES). Reason, Faith, and Duty. Sermons preached chiefly in the College Chapel. With a fine
Portrait. Square 12mo. 2.00

WEISS (JOHN). American Religion. 16mo. 1.50

WISDOM SERIES. The "Wisdom Series" will be issued
in handsome pocket volumes. 18mo. Flexible covers,
red edges.
Selections from the Apocrypha. 50
The Wisdom of Jesus, the Son of Sirach; or Ecclesias-
ticus. 50
Selections from the Thoughts of Marcus Aurelius
Antoninus. 50
Selections from the Imitation of Christ. 50
Sunshine in the Soul. Poems selected by the Editor of
"Quiet Hours." 50
Selections from Epictetus. 50
The Life and History of the Rev. Doctor John Tauler. .50
Selections from Fénelon. 50

*These books are bound in cloth, with appropriate cover
designs, mailed post-paid on receipt of price, by the publishers,
Roberts Brothers, Boston.*

CHRISTIAN HISTORY IN ITS THREE GREAT PERIODS. By Joseph Henry Allen, late lecturer on ecclesiastical history in Harvard University. Second Period. "The Middle Age." Topics.—1. The Ecclesiastical System. 2. Feudal Society. 3. The Work of Hildebrand. 4. The Crusades. 5. Chivalry. 6. The Religious Orders. 7. Heretics. 8. Scholastic Theology. 9. Religious Art. 10. Dante. 11. The Pagan Revival. Also a new edition of the First Period. "Early Christianity." Originally published under the title of "Fragments of Christian History." The two volumes uniformly bound. 16mo. Price each, . $1.25

"Whatever may be said or thought of Professor Joseph Henry Allen's 'Christian History,' which will be completed by the publication of a third volume, it is the first and foremost work of the kind ever attempted in this country. Even in our theological schools, the history of the Church is usually taught on the basis of some foreign manual, of which Guericke may be mentioned as the most favorable example, although the book is clumsy and exceedingly narrow-minded. The history of the Church, written for the use of educated men and women, has never been so much as attempted in this country. Our theologians have never been partial to ecclesiastical history, and in most cases they have been satisfied with accepting the statements of so-called standard authorities. Professor Allen's two volumes, covering the early Church and the middle age, are distinctly a new departure, for they rest in good part on original research. . . . There can be no reasonable doubt that in Professor Allen's work we have the most considerable attempt at the history of the Church ever made in the United States." — *Boston Daily Advertiser.*

Third Period. "Modern Phases." (In press.)

A NEW LIFE OF SWEDENBORG. The Life and Mission of Emanuel Swedenborg. By Benjamin Worcester. With an Introductory Chapter on Swedenborg's Place in History, an Appendix giving a complete list of Swedenborg's Writings, and a fine steel-engraved portrait and facsimile of his handwriting. One large 12mo volume. Cloth, gilt top. Price, ... $2.00.

"It is a large 12mo volume of towards five hundred pages, in which the author has collected, with great care, the leading facts relating to the Swedish seer, and has woven them into a biography prepared with scrupulous fidelity, though of course marked by the most reverent admiration for its subject. Mr. Worcester holds to the reality of the visions of Swedenborg, and believes the revelations which his works furnish as the result to be supplementary in the quality of inspiration to the Bible. The work is not one of the most attractively written pieces of biography; but its subject is interesting, and there are characteristics of Swedenborg which, aside from any supernatural endowment, plainly stamp him as one of the great minds of his time. His followers, if they are not as large as those of many of the religious sects of the day, are people of the purest minds and most intelligent perceptions, without a tendency to credulity or a tinge of fanaticism in their natures. This book will be welcomed by them as a repository of much that is valuable in the founder of their religion. It contains a portrait of Swedenborg. Many extracts from his writings are also given as incidental to the biography." — *Gazette.*

*** Our publications are for sale by all booksellers, or will be sent post-paid on receipt of advertised price.

ROBERTS BROTHERS, Boston.

Mary W. Tileston's Selections.

Quiet Hours. A Collection of Poems. Square
  16mo. First and Second Series, each $1.00
The Same. Two volumes in one. 16mo 1.50
  " "   Flexible calf 4.00
Sursum Corda. Hymns of Comfort. 16mo . . 1.25
The Blessed Life. Favorite Hymns. Square 18mo 1.00
Classic Heroic Ballads. 16mo 1.00
Daily Strength for Daily Needs: Selections for
  every day in the year. 16mo 1.00
The Same. Flexible calf or seal 3.50

WISDOM SERIES.

*Issued in handsome pocket volumes. 18mo. Flexible
covers, red edges.*

Selections from the Apocrypha . . . . $ .50
The Wisdom of Jesus, the Son of Sirach ; or, Eccle-
  siasticus 50
Selections from the Thoughts of Marcus Aurelius
  Antoninus 50
Selections from the Imitation of Christ 50
Sunshine in the Soul. First Series 50
The Same. Second Series 50
  " " Two volumes in one 75
  " " Limp calf or seal 2.50
Selections from Epictetus 50
Selections from the Life and Sermons of Tauler . . .50
Selections from Fénelon 50
Socrates. The Apology and Crito of Plato 50
  " The Phædo of Plato 50

WISDOM SERIES IN SETS.

The above in six volumes, complete, in a box. This
edition contains the entire series as far as published, including " Sunshine in the Soul." For
the set $4.50

*Sold by all booksellers. Mailed, post-paid, on receipt
of price.*

ROBERTS BROTHERS, Boston.

DAILY STRENGTH FOR DAILY NEEDS.

SELECTED BY THE EDITOR OF "QUIET HOURS."

16mo. Cloth. Price $1.00.

———◆———

" This little book is made up of selections from Scripture, and verses of poetry, and prose selections for each day of the year. We turn with confidence to any selections of this kind which Mrs. Tileston may make. In her ' Quiet Hours,' ' Sunshine for the Soul,' ' The Blessed Life,' and other works, she has brought together a large amount of rich devotional material in a poetic form. Her present book does not disappoint us. We hail with satisfaction every contribution to devotional literature which shall be acceptable to liberal Christians. This selection is made up from a wide range of authors, and there is an equally wide range of topics. It is an excellent book for private devotion or for use at the family altar." — *Christian Register.*

" It is made up of brief selections in prose and verse, with accompanying texts of Scripture, for every day in the year, arranged by the editor of ' Quiet Hours,' and for the purpose of ' bringing the reader to perform the duties and to bear the burdens of each day with cheerfulness and courage.' It is hardly necessary to say that the selection is admirably made, and that the names one finds scattered through the volume suggest the truest spiritual insight and aspiration. It is a book to have always on one's table, and to make one's daily companion." — *Christian Union.*

" They are the words of those wise and holy men, who, in all ages, have realized the full beauty of spiritual experience. They are words to comfort, to encourage, to strengthen, and to uplift into faith and aspiration. It is pleasant to think of the high and extended moral development that were possible, if such a book were generally the daily companion and counsellor of thinking men and women. Every day of the year has its appropriate text and appropriate thoughts, all helping towards the best life of the reader. Such a volume needs no appeal to gain attention to it." — *Sunday Globe, Boston.*

———

Sold by all booksellers. Mailed, post-paid, on receipt of price, by the Publishers,

ROBERTS BROTHERS, BOSTON.

QUIET HOURS.

A COLLECTION OF POEMS, MEDITATIVE AND RELIGIOUS.

FIRST AND SECOND SERIES.

" Such a book as this seems to us much better adapted than any formal book of devotion to beget a calm and prayerful spirit in the reader. It will no doubt become a dear companion to many earnestly religious people." — *Christian Register.*

"Thousands of thoughtful and devout minds have been helped, comforted, and strengthened by the little volume of poetical selections, published under the title of ' Quiet Hours,' some years since ; and these and many more will welcome a new volume, published under the same title, constructed on the same plan, and breathing the same earnest and gentle spirit. This second series of ' Quiet Hours,' like the first, bears the imprint of Roberts Bros. It is contained in a dainty little volume of the Little Classic style, prettily printed and bound ; and there are not far from two hundred pieces in it, grouped under the heads, ' Nature,' ' Morning and Evening,' ' Inward Strife,' ' Life and Duty,' ' Prayer and Aspiration,' ' Trust and Adoration,' ' Heaven and the Saints,' and ' Miscellaneous.' The poems are chosen with exquisite taste ; their range is broad, and their tone is clear and true." — *Boston Journal.*

" 'Quiet Hours ' is the appropriate title which some unnamed compiler has given to a collection of musings of many writers, — a nosegay made up of some slighter, choicer, and more delicate flowers from the garden of the poets. Emerson, Chadwick, Higginson, Arnold, Whittier, and Clough are represented, as well as Coleridge, Browning, Wordsworth, and Tennyson ; and the selections widely vary in character, ranging from such as relate to the moods and aspects of nature, to voices of the soul when most deeply stirred." — *Congregationalist.*

18mo, cloth, red edges. Price, $1.00 each. Two vols. in one. Price, $1.50 ; calf or seal, $4.00. Sold by all booksellers. Mailed post-paid, by the Publishers,

ROBERTS BROTHERS,
BOSTON

www.ingramcontent.com/pod-product-compliance
Lightning Source LLC
Chambersburg PA
CBHW020117030726
47498CB00006B/2151